SIMPLY BE

MW01117967

"*Simply Because We Are Human* is a collection of the writer's honest interactions with mental illness. The descriptive, poetic memories and vignettes trace her understanding, acceptance, and the barriers she tried to run away from. Her story is both common and exceptional, and dares to expose her journey to mental health wide open to the light."

—**Amy Pendino,** author of
The Witness Tree and *Wild Horses*

"This swift and dexterous memoir lays bare the challenges and triumphs of effective mental health treatment. Bracing, sensitive, and savvy, *Simply Because We Are Human* shares hard-won lessons along with a vigorous dose of inspiration."

—**James Cihlar**, author of *The Shadowgraph*

"*Simply Because We Are Human* is a vivid, moving narrative that takes a deeper look into the experience of living with clinical depression. This is a great read for those looking to educate themselves on clinical depression, and young people currently wading through the dark waters of the disease."

—**Evelyn Louise May**, founder and editor,
Other Worldly Women Press

Simply Because We Are Human

SIMPLY BECAUSE
WE ARE HUMAN

A Memoir

K. J. JOSEPH

ISBN 13: 978-1-63489-412-8

Library of Congress Catalog Number has been applied for.
Printed in the United States of America
First Printing: 2021

25 24 23 22 21   5 4 3 2 1

Cover design by Michelle Williamson
Interior design by Patrick Maloney

Wise Ink Creative Publishing
807 Broadway St NE
Suite 46
Minneapolis, MN, 55413

In memory of Matt Pelant

TABLE OF CONTENTS

ACKNOWLEDGMENTS

When a friend of mine in high school committed suicide at seventeen years old, I could not help but feel I needed to break my own silence about having a mental illness. I had no idea my friend was depressed, but at the same time, nobody knew I struggled with clinical depression. It was not something that was talked about often. So I started to chisel away at the barrier I had built around myself to shield my darkness from the world. Bit by bit I continued to expose more about my mental illness. I started by talking to my high school friends about my depression. I haven't stopped communicating about it since. I wanted to write my story, but for a long time I found myself unable to get the words that I wanted onto the page.

It was not until years later—after I married my best friend and the love of my life, Noah—that my stepdaughter inspired me to revisit the project of writing about my experiences dealing with clinical depression. She had decided to write about mental health and social stigma for her eighth-grade capstone paper. In her paper, titled "Reduce the Stigma," she writes,

Mental health stigma has been around since the ancient world and still continues today. For my capstone project, I chose to research how society can reduce the stigma and help create a more inclusive environment for everyone. History, types of stigma, causes, the effect it has on people, organizations and religion all play a role in the stigmatization seen every day. The lack of equal opportunity caused by stigma about people with mental illnesses will start to decline by educating the public.

Talking with my stepdaughter about her paper recaptured that desire I had inside me to tell my story in hopes of helping others. For that reason, I must send her a huge thank-you for sending that spark of inspiration my direction.

Also, to my husband, stepson, and stepdaughter, a huge thank-you for being my supportive rock while I took so much time out of our lives to work on this project. Finally, my parents, who are my greatest fans: my dad, mom, stepdad, and stepmom. Thank you for putting up with me all those years. You are the people who created me into the person I am today. I love you.

K. J. Joseph

INTRODUCTION

In *The Art of Memoir*, Mary Karr states, "No matter how self-aware you are, memoir wrenches at your insides precisely because it makes you battle with your very self—your neat analyses and tidy excuses." When I finally sat down and decided to start writing *Simply Because We Are Human*, I thought I was self-aware when it came to my mental illness. I ignorantly believed I was completely prepared to write about the emotional complications related to my depression.

I was so wrong.

As I dug deeper into my writing craft, I realized just how many roadblocks I had to break down to find the heart and soul of my story. There were numerous occasions when my words would be flowing and then I would hit a complete dead end. When I took a step back from myself, I was able to understand that my dead ends were my own personal self-defense mechanism. The blockades consistently appeared when I was writing about a more personally difficult part of my life. Thankfully, I was able to challenge my craft and push through by researching other writers' work that dealt with difficult topics. With these writers' past knowledge, I was able to utilize the tools I needed in order to write about my own difficult topics and produce my graduate craft paper, titled "Grief Memoir and the Emotional Link: Narrative Distance, Chronological, and Nonchronological Narrative." These instruments were crucial in the completion of my memoir.

Memoirists expose the raw, vulnerable truths in life in order to connect to themselves, their readers, and to the world around them. In the case of *Simply Because We Are Human,* my goal is to continue to knock down barriers that lie between communication and the darkness of mental illness. Even if the outcome of this work ends up only removing one brick in the barrier, I will have done what I set out to do. So many people's lives are lost to the hopelessness that consumes a person's existence because of mental illness.

We need to do better as a world.

There is an invisible pact that memoirists have with their readers regarding truth. Sure, it would be great to paint a picture of perfection when writing about my own life. That is just not realistic. Nobody has a perfect life. If I decide to skip through the difficult parts of my story because I am having a hard time reliving them, then I am failing my audience. This is what Karr means when she says "neat analyses and tidy excuses." If I didn't get the rawness of the story I set out to tell on the page, I would feel I was failing my readers.

Truth comes along with an author's ability to piece

together memory and research, but most importantly, truth is produced with an author's willingness to pull at the loose thread to completely unravel, expose, and embrace any unexpected discoveries. Karr says, "Memory is a pinball in a machine—it messily ricochets around between image, idea, fragments of scenes, stories you've heard. Then the machine goes tilt and snaps off. But most of the time, we keep memories packed away. I sometimes liken that moment of sudden unpacking to circus clowns pouring out of a miniature car trunk—how did so much fit into such a small space?"

Writing my personal story about clinical depression has been every emotion wrapped into one package topped off with a big red bow. What started out as a dream of mine became words on scattered pages and over time transformed into a draft, which I later ignorantly discovered was barely brushing across the surface of my own life story. The ability to dust out every corner of my soul to tell my story has been a life-changing experience. My hope is that my story helps others and plays a role in chiseling away the barriers that limit the evolution of communication when it comes to mental illness.

Thank you,

K. J. Joseph

"To be in a clinical depression is to experience a third dimension in which you are still technically alive but incapable of living."

—Paul Gruchow
Letters to a Young Madman: A Memoir

Chapter One

THIRD DIMENSION

It was a scenic, warm Wisconsin day as my boyfriend Nick and I made the drive from La Crosse to Black River Memorial Hospital. The back roads wove tightly between the plush green bluffs that contrasted with the blue afternoon sky. The clouds appeared to be manipulated by the rays of sunlight to spotlight nature's stage. We had done this drive together many times before, only today was different. The route was the same, but there was nothing familiar about the destination.

Nick calmly sat in the driver's seat. He was wearing his favorite black Tool T-shirt and tattered Brewers hat that he put on over his unkempt hair, which he refused to cut no matter how much anyone, including me, pressured him. It was like he believed he would lose part of himself by having to conform to society's demands of being a clean-cut individual working a nine-to-five office job. Nick was, and still is, a rock drummer to the core of his soul. He had the drumming skills, only he never played a stage that would give him the exposure he needed to make a living out of it.

Nick drove with the windows down. I usually loved when

the breeze brushed across my face, but at that moment it was irritating. It felt as if I was being overstimulated, like a constant itch that, when scratched, only became worse. The only sounds I could hear were the Stone Temple Pilots on the stereo and the wind. They were no longer the usual pleasant sounds. It was like someone had turned up the volume on everything. In the haze of my illness, I found myself resenting the concept of time. I wanted to shut off the world around me like a TV or hit the pause button on my DVD player. Only I was all too familiar with the fact that time moves forward without any sympathy.

The roads between La Crosse and Black River Falls usually made me feel at ease because being away from work and everyday life gave me room to breathe. Every other time we had driven that stretch, the road refueled my soul much like my lungs distributed oxygen to the limbs of my body. Nature's surroundings had a way of melting the tension out of my muscles attached to my bones as I exhaled farther from civilization.

Now every push and pull of my body was a fight, a struggle, simply because my mind was in distress. My connection to God or the universe was practically nonexistent. I peered out from the passenger window to see the same scenic landscape, but I could not enjoy the beauty. I was tangled in nature's vines, strangled, my rotting carcass left for some random hiker to find years later to finish my story. I was in so much physical, mental, and spiritual pain, it was all I could do to fight the urge to jump out of the moving car.

Nick knew that I had experienced clinical depression in the past, but this was his first time witnessing one of my episodes. The noise of hopeless negativity was taking over the stream of consciousness inside my head, causing me to fold into myself, becoming trapped. Everyday tasks like getting out of bed in the morning, showering, or eating a meal became a struggle in my world.

Nick was my best friend. We had been friends for years before we'd become a couple. We had lived together in La Crosse for the past two years and had been a couple for about three. During that time, I hadn't had any major episodes, until now. I did not expect him to make things right for me, but I expected him to support me. He did the best he could at the time, and I am sure it was exceedingly difficult to support me because I was still struggling to come to grips with the reality of my illness and what long-term treatment looked like for me.

I did not have the capacity to process large-scale items at that moment. I appreciated that he was driving me to the hospital, but at the end of the day, there was nothing he could do for me but be there. I had to make the choices to help myself. From what I gathered, Nick was not crazy about medication and therapy when treating mental illness. He seemed to think that if there was something wrong, there was a logical, situational reason for it. Therefore, I was less likely to talk about my mental illness around him.

Some people I knew over the years believed that medication was taking the easy way out and that a person should be able to manage mental illness naturally. I am not saying this approach can't work for certain individuals, because it can. What I am saying is everyone's situation is different. "Naturally" did not work for me.

Clinical depression impacts much of my life and is a part of who I am. I never expect people to fully understand or fix me, but I did expect the person who I marry and surround myself with for the rest of my life to acknowledge the personal reality of what my mental illness was and how I treated it.

I was thankful that at that moment in time Nick was not in a talking mood. I found it comforting not to speak. At that point, conversation was such a forced effort for me. I could not push out my internal pain to talk about music, the next show he was going to drum at, or the camping trip we wanted to go on. None of that mattered. Frankly, I did not have the ability to care about anything; caring about myself was difficult enough. I had to focus on fighting off the negative thoughts. All my energy went to reminding myself who I was. I knew that if I did not get help soon, my mental illness would kill me.

Daydreaming of taking my own life was a recurring theme. Suicidal thoughts were not something I shared with anyone at that time. I was denying the reality of my illness. I did not want to accept that my mental illness was something that I would always have to manage and take medication for.

Earlier that week I found myself standing alone in my kitchen with a knife pressed to the skin on my vulnerable wrist. I even thought about how I needed to make sure the blade was aligned with the tubes of blood that lay underneath my translucent skin to ensure my termination. I was not thinking about anyone in my life or who it would hurt. All I was thinking of was how I wanted the horrible pain to stop, even if it meant ending my life. I was barely present in my own body anymore.

When I found myself standing in the kitchen with a knife, contemplating cutting into the skin of my wrists, I knew that I had to get help soon or I would eventually lose complete control. This was not the first time I had been through a depressive episode or thought about death. In fact, I had been dealing with this off and on since I was eight years old. Only this time it was worse than it had ever been. In the past I did not experience such a drastic drop to depression. This incident was a wake-up call, a red flag, and a smack in the face. It ingrained a fear that will forever haunt my soul as a reminder not to let myself falter ever again from the things I can control.

It had been a little less than two years since I stopped taking my meds this time around. In the past, I had gone two or three times as many years without my medication while remaining fine. Despite the times I consulted my doctor to stop medication, I always seemed to come back to a drastic dip in depression. Due to the large gaps in my life without needing medication, the thought was I would not always need to be on medication. I was pushing for this, as I did not want to rely on medication.

The truth is that I wanted to believe that not being on medication was possible. I never was a fan of taking any medication unless needed. I felt the healthiest the years that I was balanced and not on medication, because it always had side effects. Side effects took time to adjust to, and who knew what the long-term effects would be.

So on that spring car ride as I sat in misery, again, it was becoming quite clear that not being on medication was not an option for me. There was no way to predict if I would be fine for eight years or one. This was something that I would be dealing with for the rest of my life. I was so angry at myself for letting it get this far . . . again.

Clinical depression made me hide like a turtle retracting

into its shell. It was not that I did not care. The problem was that my mental illness made it impossible for me to care. As I sat in the passenger seat of Nick's car, I simply existed. It was as if I were meshed into the upholstery. In fact, I might as well have been an inanimate object, like the rearview mirror just watching the world go by me.

There was absolutely nothing anyone could say to me to make me feel better in the state of mind I was in. No words can take away a chemical imbalance of the brain; only medication can do that. I needed to be put back on medication. My past encounters with depression provided me with a single thread of hope that was dwindling fast: I knew what medication worked for me, and if I took my medication, I could get better. I had done it before. The problem was that, because of my depression, the realization was just a fleeting glimpse. I had a hard time remembering what it was like to be better while I was in the thick of the dark woods, but I held onto that single thread tethering my soul to my body as tightly as I could. My life depended on it.

I knew that my self-awareness would completely vanish if I was without medication for long enough. Eventually, my mental illness would consume my reality and take over my sanity, like trying to gather dandelion fuzz in the wind. I would be trapped inside a corner of my own mind, watching everything happen to me but unable to do anything. I pictured this fragile thread connecting my soul to my body, and for once I could not blame anything or anyone but myself. I was terrified. There I was, winding through some of the most beautiful back roads of the Midwest, listening to my favorite music, next to my boyfriend, and I could only see death.

Chapter Two

A DARK SPRING

If my depression were a season, it would be the first weeks of spring. The blanket of snow melts, revealing a smorgasbord of forgotten items lying amongst the yard waste from the previous season. The ice containing decomposed leaves melts, presenting a soup of mold and mildew that gives off a ripe stench in the air. I lace up my running shoes in retaliation. My front yard, mushy beneath my feet like an overabsorbed sponge, leaves my running shoes caked with mud. I struggle to reach the street despite mud's disapproval as it suctions the soles of my shoes to stop them dead in their tracks.

I push forward, almost leaving a shoe stuck in the muck, and feel a relief as I cross over to the pavement with both shoes still on. I am lighter now as nothing is weighing me down. I wind around the neighborhood streets mindful of Mother Nature's winter leftovers, potholes, and asphalt chunks. The thought of a sprained ankle or twisted knee is motivation enough to stay focused on my footing.

Once I leave the residential area and hit the main street, I can hear traffic up ahead before I can see any evidence of it. As I approach the intersection, I can hear a loud system booming rap in the SUV that is stopped at the light. As I run by, I pretend not to notice the driver dancing. It isn't long before I cross the intersection that traffic starts darting by. The vehicles' tires speed through the puddles and splash soupy remnants toward the sidewalk where I am running. The watery, sandy mixture goes flying onto my jacket and jogging pants as if the universe is trying to warn me to turn back. I am stubborn, and this only makes me more determined to continue forward. I try to focus on the bridge up ahead that crosses over the busy highway. I convince myself not to give up by remembering once I reach the overpass, I will be back in a residential area and away from this traffic.

Once I reach the bridge, I hear the whoosh of passing traffic below as I jog over Highway 169. I can't help but think about all the cars that pass underneath me as I make my way across. How many people are in those cars? Do any of them know me? I bet it will be the only time that most of those people will ever cross my path. I wonder about all the stories that lie in each vehicle that darts under me. Does anyone feel the clinical depression as I do? Are any of those passengers out driving to take a break from all the chaos? Are they going on a trip, or are they just out for usual errands? I know I will never know, but it does not stop me from wondering each time I run over any highway.

I leave behind the few blocks of residential area after the

bridge to make it to the trail that traces Medicine Lake. By now I am constantly playing leapfrog over the puddles that have formed along this tarred trail. I can't hurdle over many due to their size, and the dirty mix of water absorbs into my athletic socks, squishing water out of my shoes with each new step forward. It will not be long before my feet are soaked and numb.

The air is thick with pollen. I crave the cool breath of winter that feels fresh and clean, because now, I must make sure not to inhale the fuzz or dust. That would send me into a coughing fit and would surely end my run.

The lake has not completely melted yet, leaving the gray slush along the shoreline. A collage of garbage has washed up from the ice fishermen and fisherwomen of the season. The trash is showcased against the muddy brown colors that have taken over the landscape, making the area look abandoned and dumpy.

By now I am in my runner's rhythm, and I start to focus on how everything around me is struggling to come back to life. The heavy white layer of snow that wraps around Mother Earth like a quilted blanket through winter, comforting her, is now removed, exposing the barren branches of bones to the cool air.

The process of nature coming back to life is in motion. The tulip will bud and fight to break through the ground's surface, reaching for the sunlight. The pavement will once again be dry as the moisture nourishes the plants and covers the naked tree branches with thick green leaves. The fuzz and pollen will not linger and will be replaced by the smell of lilac and an array of colorful flowers.

As I finish running by the lake, I turn off the path to head toward home, and I see a gaggle of geese fly overhead toward the lake. With lots of honking and splashing, they land together, settling into a calm float as if they just returned home after their long migration. I am reminded that through every dark, twisted change in life comes a new beginning. Spring fights to bring forth new life and beauty. I fight my depression to bring forth my soulfulness and happiness. The seasons change with Mother Earth's fight, and so do I.

Chapter Three

SEVENTY-FIVE CENTS

My passion for running started at my mom's family reunion when I was five years old. We were at the Fourth of July carnival in Amasa, Michigan, a small town right outside Crystal Falls. The barbeque smell made my stomach rumble in hunger. Kids were running around everywhere with sparklers and waving little American flags.

A pudgy middle-aged woman in a lavender dress waddled over to me and asked if I wanted to join the footrace. I glanced over to my mom and younger sister Courtney for their approval.

"Go ahead, Kris," said my mom.

"Yeah, yeah, do it," my little sister said, jumping up and down with excitement.

My first reaction was to say no. Sure, I wanted to make my sister and mother proud. But I was a shy child, and I had never done a footrace before. Then I recall looking over at Grandma Ellen, standing next to my mother with her short, tightly wound brown curls and red lips, and I knew that I had to run because I wanted to make my grandma proud.

Since as long as I can remember, I have heard the stories

about how my grandmother was a woman before her time. She enlisted in the Navy WAVE and was in the first class of women to graduate from Aviation Machinist's Mate School located at Naval Air Station Memphis in Tennessee. People were always telling her she could not do certain things because she was female, and she would turn around and show them that she could. One of the things she was known for was being an amazing athlete. She would even beat the boys. I wanted to show her that I, too, could be an athlete.

Still, I was not quite sure about it. There were lots of little kids my age, but there were also some kids who looked much older and more experienced. I envisioned myself shrinking by the second like Alice does in *Alice in Wonderland* when she drinks the potion. I joined the group without letting myself think about it too much. I wanted to be brave.

The pudgy woman in the lavender dress gathered us all in a field on the edge of the carnival. An elderly lady who looked like she was dressed for Sunday church stood at the starting line. I remember thinking to myself that if she was dressed up so fancy for this event, it must be a bigger deal than I thought. This only made me more nervous. It took a while to get all the kids rounded up even with the assistance of all the parents.

Before I knew it, I was lined up at the starting line, wondering what I'd gotten myself into. The Sunday church lady yelled, "Ready . . . set . . . go!" The race was off to an un-gracefully slow start for our group. Most kids looked to their parents for guidance on what to do. I was one of them. I looked to my mom and started slowly jogging with uncertainty. Many of the others started running toward their parents. Some did not even move the entire time. A little girl near me started crying. I passed one little girl playing with a flower as her mom attempted to direct her to run forward.

After a few moments of jogging hesitantly, I was off. A tall older girl with long dark curls was already in the lead, and I was determined not to let her get too far ahead. I could see the line of ribbon that two ladies were holding up as posed statues in the near distance. *Aha*, I thought. The finish line.

Now I was so focused on my goal to get to that finish line that all the distraction and nervousness melted away. I felt lighter than air as I began to move faster and faster to the end. Those hundred meters felt like an eternity. I could hear my parents and sisters yelling my name. "Go, go, Kris!" I passed the finish with excitement in second place.

My family, including my grandma Ellen, was so proud of me. I was so proud of myself. I received seventy-five cents for winning second place. In my five-year-old mind, the money immediately turned into the amount of candy I could buy. I remember most of all that my little sister was more excited for me than I was for myself, and she could not wait to come over to give me a hug. I had never seen anyone so proud of me as she was that day.

My mom insisted on getting a picture of the two of us. In the picture you can see me grinning as I hold up my three quarters. My little sister has her arm around me. She has her head held high and her shoulders back. It's as if being the sister of the girl who won second place in the footrace made her the sister of a celebrity. To her, my placing in the footrace really meant something.

My mom framed this picture along with my three quarters, and it hung in my childhood home for years until that the picture was handed down to me. I reframed it and placed it on my living room shelf, where the story could live on for my family. I still have those three quarters.

I was much too young at the time to realize how significant that first footrace was for me. It was the beginning of a lifelong relationship that would save my life.

Chapter Four

THE UNKNOWN REASON

As I sat barely holding myself together in the passenger seat of my boyfriend's car, I forced myself to focus on anything other than emotional pain. I found myself going back to the first time depression decided to pay me an unexpected visit. It was 1989. I was eight years old, attending third grade at Vista View Elementary School in Burnsville, Minnesota. Back then I was still stuck on the fact that boys had cooties and concerned about whether I would have enough time in the morning to crimp my hair before school.

That day, one minute I was leaning against the brick wall outside my classroom and talking to my friends, and then the next minute this negative, fearful force started to consume my entire existence. Nothing awful had happened to me that day to make me feel horrible. It was not something I could comprehend or explain at that early age. I just knew every inch of my body felt intense grief and the only thing I could do was cry.

Crying in front of people outside of my immediate family was one of the worst things that could happen to my third-grade self. I hated when the attention was on me even when

23

I was not upset. I was a very shy kid. My friends were all huddled around me.

"Kris, what's wrong?"

"Are you okay?"

"What happened, Kris?"

I had no answers. I did not know what was happening to me, and that only made me more upset. In the middle of all the chaos, I came up with the best answer I could think of.

"My stomach hurts and I don't feel good!"

I cried and held onto my stomach for dear life. One of my friends confided in one of the nearby lunch ladies, who instructed her to walk me to the nurse's office down the hall. Without hesitation, my friend linked her arm through mine and started to half walk, half skip me to the nurse's office, reassuring me that everything would be okay and the nurse would know what to do. I sobbed the entire time. I could not stop. By the time my friend left me with the nurse, I could not break the tears enough to tell her what was wrong.

I can still feel the iciness of the nurse's office. The only time I had been to the nurse was during the tour at the beginning of each new year, when our class would walk around the building to meet all our teachers and staff. The nurse's office smelled like the medicine my mom sprayed on my cuts that caused a painful sting. The entire room was an off-white that had yellowed over time, and the bright florescent lights only enhanced the room's aging. I sat in one of the uncomfortable wooden chairs as that nurse handed me a box of tissues and interrogated me.

"What is wrong now, deary?"

Through the tears and short breaths, I was able to force out the words one syllable at a time through the cries.

"My—

"stom—

"ach—

"hurts?"

The nurse scratched her head and smiled at me calmly. She grabbed a paper cup from the nearby water cooler and handed it to me.

"Kris, when did it start hurting?"

I took the water but was only able to hold onto it as I attempted to answer the question between struggling breaths.

"J-Just

"be—

"fore—

"l-lunch."

Her hair was a copper brown and badly permed, and it rested in a triangular shape on the top of her head. Her beady eyes were peeking through her wavy bangs, enhancing her already obvious mad-scientist look.

"Well having a stomachache isn't fun. Did you eat or drink anything earlier today that you usually don't eat?"

Now she had her hands on her hips, and I could hardly make out her face through the blurred tears of vision.

"N-no."

I felt her cool, bony hand on my forehead as she took a thermometer out and placed it in my mouth. For some reason, the focus of keeping the thermometer under my tongue was distraction enough to help me start to calm down.

"Does anything else hurt? Do you have a cough or sore throat?"

I shook my head no. Then she grabbed the thermometer out of my mouth pulled it up to her face as she squinted to read it.

"No temperature."

She looked at me with a puzzled look. Once she realized that she could not find anything wrong with me, the real interrogation started.

"Did anything happen today? Were any of the kids teasing you or mean to you?"

By then I had calmed down as was holding a ball of tissue in my hand dabbing my eyes.

"No."

The nurse picked up the nearby trash can and leaned it in my direction so I could toss the tissues in it.

"What about at home?"

"Do you feel safe at home?"

"Any changes?"

I swallowed hard and took a deep breath. "Nobody was mean to me, and things are safe at home."

Now I was beyond frustrated. I did not want to tell her my parents were getting divorced. I didn't think that was why I was upset, and I knew she would blame it all on that. She would decide that she had figured out that the underlining cause of my distress was the divorce and I was too young to comprehend it.

"No changes at home?"

The tears were flowing again. I knew I was going to have to tell her. "Well, my parents are getting divorced."

That was true, but I didn't think that was the reason to why I was feeling this way.

"Oh, I'm so sorry, dear."

As she leaned in for a hug, I could tell she genuinely felt for me. At that time there was only one other person I knew who had divorced parent. From my lens, divorce wasn't common in my school or neighborhood.

"Well, let me call your mother to come get you."

She turned to pick up the phone and dialed the number off my student chart, which she had pulled out at some point through my panic. I was frustrated more than anything. Nothing she asked matched what I was going through, and that made me more disconnected. I wanted to tell her exactly what was going on, but I could not explain the feeling. It was so unfamiliar. What was I going to say—that an evil alien bubble of energy decided to randomly enter my body? They would lock me up for sure.

The truth was that I had no comprehension of what was going on. I literally did not have the emotional maturity to fully understand. By the time the nurse reached my mother on the other end of the line, my stomach did hurt because of how upset I was.

"Your mom will be here in twenty minutes to come get you. Are you okay to sit and relax here until she arrives?"

I finally drank the water and attempted to fully calm my breath down. The nurse picked up the trash can once more and leaned in my direction as I tossed the cup into it.

"Yes, and thank you."

I leaned back in my chair and folded my arms. I thought about how this would put my mom in a last-minute predicament of finding someone to teach her class for the rest of the day. It was not easy to find a substitute to take over the class. I quickly forgot about that, as my current emotional state was all consuming.

As I sat in that wooden chair in the nurse's office, confined to my saddened body, I was afraid. I did not know what was going on. I could usually explain my feelings. I finally was able to take a deep breath to feel a brief sense of relief, knowing my mom was on her way.

Chapter Five

BIG RED

During the two weeks leading up to my first appointment with a mental health professional, I experienced at least three more days much like the first time my mother had to pick me up at the nurse's office. The hopeless feeling came out of nowhere, without warning, and that was enough to add an uneasiness to my usual school day.

I was not looking forward to going to an appointment. The word *psychiatrist* was something I only learned about from movies, television shows, and cartoons. The loony, crazy person who was not right in the head. I preferred to look at it as a doctor for people going through problems. The thing was, after everything I had endured the past weeks, I still didn't want to go to the psychiatrist. I dreaded going, and the anticipation just added to my already difficult mood.

When I arrived at the office, there were no books, toys, or magazines for anyone of my age. The magazines available were about cars, cooking, and gardening. They did not even have a tank of colorful fish to watch like they had at my typical doctor and dentist office. So I decided to just sit next to my mother, patiently waiting for the receptionist to call my name.

The large rectangular room had two squared-off sections of chairs, each with its own coffee table piled with boring magazines. The waiting room was dark red and cream. Even the abstract wall art matched the awful combination of colors. I always loved art, but I quickly decided my baby sister could have painted something better. The red made me think of fresh cherries that my mother would buy us to eat for snacks in summertime. I particularly liked them because we could spit out the pits when we were outside. My sister and I challenged each other to see how far we could spit the seeds.

It was not long before the praying mantis of a receptionist opened the waiting room door and called out my name as she peered over the top of her eyeglasses.

"Kris Berg," she said with her nasally voice.

I heard my name, but I froze in place. For some reason, I had hoped that they would skip right over me and I could be on my way. When I did not respond, my mother nudged me, and I stood up immediately.

"I'm right here," I said. "I'm Kris."

The mantis lady turned her head in my direction. "Hi, Kris. Follow me this way."

My mom and I both got up and headed to the door. The mantis lady pushed her dark-framed glasses back up on the ridge of her nose.

"I'm sorry, the doctor will first see Kris by herself and then later will talk to you."

My mother looked in my direction to confirm that I was okay with this, and I hesitantly nodded in agreement. She reluctantly returned to her seat. By that time, my wild imagination had fully kicked in to distract me. I had myself following a green, human-size praying mantis with glasses down a long hallway. What child would not be terrified at that image?

To my relief, the hallway was warmly lit and much more welcoming than the waiting room. As I followed Mantis around a right-hand corner, the hallway was illuminated solely by the sun that peered in through the long windows on both sides of the red-and-white checkered tile floors. At the end of the hallway was a large, dark mahogany door displaying my fate. I could not believe how much the door stuck out against all the rays of sunshine peeking through the massive windows. It appeared to be a door to another dimension or universe.

To take my mind off the door of final destination, I peered out the windows on both sides of me. My eyes were drawn to the cleanly cut, brilliant green hedges that outlined the windows. To the left, there was a fountain that trickled clean, clear water over smooth pebbles. There were flowers of all kinds exhibiting a palette full of striking colors.

Much to my luck, I had recently watched my favorite movie at the time, *Labyrinth*. So my mind naturally went to the maze of hedges that wove outside the castle. Only I knew that behind that intimidating door I would not find David Bowie in his glitter and spandex. Behind that door was unknown territory for me, but at least for that brief moment my creative mind was able to ease my nerves.

Mantis grabbed the handle of the door that I had already decided by its appearance would be very heavy and creak open slowly to reveal a dramatic, mysterious creature.

Of course, nothing remotely close to that happened, and reality hit me immediately, taking away all the suspense that I had built up in my head. Once I was inside the office, Mantis introduced me to Dr. Lippy.

"Dr. Lippy, this is your new intake, Kris."

Dr. Lippy sat behind her massive wooden desk. She was middle aged and wrinkly, and her voice sounded as if she smoked three packs a day. Her wiry, wild black hair made her look unkempt and crazy. The stench of stale cigarettes lingered in the air. It reminded me of sitting near the smoking section on an airplane. I hated that smell. It took forever to get the stench out of my nostrils and clothes.

"Well, hello, Kris. Nice to meet you."

As I took a moment to collect myself, Mantis lady handed the doctor my file with what could only be one of her six legs.

Then Mantis motioned to the red leather armchair designed for a giant that rested right in front of the doctor's desk. With a shocked look, I started to climb the mountain of a chair reaching the top to meet Dr. Lippy's judgmental eyes.

She seemed to be getting lankier and more mantis-like by the minute. I shook my head to stop my mind from spinning, but by then I had already had her in my mind wearing a crown as queen of the praying mantises.

"Nice to meet you too," I said with a smile as Mantis closed the door behind her with a heavy thump, taking my imagination along with it.

Dr. Lippy looked at me like I was an alien from another planet with three eyes. It did not help that I felt as tiny as a doll sitting in the middle of a ridiculously large chair. I must have looked as awkward as I felt. My body barely took up a quarter of the seat, and my feet dangled way above the floor. I focused on the weight of my feet to distract myself from the nervousness, and I swayed them back and forth.

The room was similar to how I pictured it. It even had a deep brown leather couch in the middle with a chair next to it. I immediately pictured myself lying on that couch, rambling on while the doctor sat in the chair taking notes. What would she think about my theory that I was destined to marry Joey McIntyre from New Kids on the Block? I mean, I knew that it sounded crazy, but it was going to happen.

The entire office smelled of wood and embodied sophistication. The dark wood desk sat like a throne over the entire room.

"Miss Kris, I hear that you are having a hard time at school lately," Dr. Lippy said with a voice that gave me the urge to clear my throat.

"Yes." I could barely get the word out. My mouth was now dry, and I was becoming smaller and smaller by the minute. I was beginning to think I would disappear completely.

"Can you tell me what happened?" Dr. Lippy said. By that time, she had already opened my file and had her pen ready to take notes.

I focused on the weight of my feet as they dangled back and forth.

"I don't know. I keep having these horrible feelings that make me cry," I said.

"Is there anyone bullying you at school?" she asked.

I shook my head.

"Do you have friends and feel like you belong?"

I nodded.

"Are you doing well in school?"

I nodded again.

Dr. Lippy sat up and leaned over her desk. She wanted to make sure that I had her full attention. She cleared her raspy throat.

"Now, Kristine, this is a safe space. Is there anything going on at home that is making you feel sad? Is anyone hurting you at home? You can tell me, and everything will be okay."

"No," I said. "I feel safe at home." I crossed my arms. "Like I told the nurse at school, nobody is sexually abusing me or beating me up."

Dr. Lippy sat up even straighter now folding her hands on her desk.

"Kristine, I have to ask, and it's okay to tell me if anything is happening. I know it can be scary."

"Nothing is happening to me at home." I spoke louder this time. "I'm happy at home."

Dr. Lippy scribbled some notes down on my file. I felt very insecure about her recording my every move. I could not help but wonder what she was writing. I had already feared that she was diagnosing me as some insane eight-year-old. She looked down from her huge desk at me as if I was part of a circus freak show, her eyebrows raised and eyes wide as if she had been watching the amazing bearded lady. I already felt like a weirdo, and this was making me feel even worse.

"Kristine, your mother mentioned that she and your father are in the process of getting a divorce. Do you think that has anything to do with how you might be feeling?"

"No. In fact, I get to see my dad more and I like my dad's new friend," I said.

Dr. Lippy smirked a bit. I did not think I had said anything funny. I gave her a confused look. She just continued to jot notes in her notebook for a minute while I sat there confused.

She set her pen down and closed my file.

"Kristine, I'm going to take you out to the waiting room and then talk to your mother for a few minutes. Do you have any questions for me?"

I had so many questions. Was I crazy? What were they going to do to me? Would they lock me up and have me wear one of those crazy jackets? Instead I just looked at her and shook my head.

"Okay, Kristine, then let me take you to the waiting room."

I nodded, and by that point I was just relieved it was over. I had to awkwardly scoot myself to the front of Big Red to get to my feet. I felt embarrassed. I followed Dr. Lippy out the door and felt a little lighter as I entered the glass hallway of the labyrinth, allowing my imagination to return once more.

Chapter Six

SAFEKEEPING

A solid foundation is just below my running shoes. It's a black asphalt path that first hugs up between the nearby lake and then farther down splits between the woods of Minnesota. In spring it's full of puddles that I hurdle over as the fuzz of blossoms tickles my skin. I breathe in my favorite smell: fresh lilacs.

In summer, the heat visibly rises off the path in a distant mirage. The heat beating off the path of tar keeps me wondering if the bottom of my shoes will melt off. Fall breezes scatter dead leaves that crunch underneath my feet. The winter blankets winding curves with a mixture of snow and ice that makes me cautious with every step I take. The air is pure and cool as I drink it in and breathe it out.

This path welcomes me when I need time to myself. I visit my friend through every season. I discover a poetic rhythm with each step I take. My movement allows me to get out of my head like a form of meditation. My steps are a beat to my drum, a repetition to my heart. It is a magical percussion that calms my spiraling mind. I easily focus on the soul and experience peace.

Out on the path, I am surrounded by nature. It's my time. I don't think about my responsibilities and deadlines. I rarely come across other people but might pass by a deer, fox, or chipmunk. I hear the chirping of birds and possible clack of the woodpecker cheering me on. The only race is with myself, and with each act of movement I feel lighter with the release of stress. This path is a place that I can count on. It is a place to call my own.

Chapter Seven

THIRTEEN

After my visit to the first psychiatrist in third grade, I was sent to a child psychologist, whom I regularly visited. After the first experience, I wasn't expecting much from this new place. Let me just say, as an eight-year-old kid, I would have been thrilled to just have some color in the room. That all changed as soon as I walked into a lobby that lit up like a candy store. The office had a fish tank, kid magazines, and toys to play with. Also, believe it or not, there were other kids. It was right up my alley.

My therapist had long brown hair and flowing skirts, and she smelled kind of funny. She was what my mother called a flower child or hippie. I did not quite understand what that meant until I was older, but I looked forward to her quirky personality. We played with games and toys while we talked. I didn't understand why she talked to me like I was a complete baby, but I just went with it because I was happy to not go back to the last psychiatrist. I didn't understand how playing with toys and games was going to help me, but somewhere along the way I started to get better.

Eventually, the depressive episodes left as suddenly as they had come on. There was no explanation as to why. My therapist thought I was a healthy child and that it might have been an isolated incident. Maybe the divorce was a trigger for what was much later in my life diagnosed as clinical depression. I could not tell you for certain. I am not a doctor or expert in psychology. All I knew at the time was that I felt better and, as an eight-year-old kid, I did not think much about it.

The next four years brought lots of change, as time typically does for everyone. My best friends, who lived down the block from me, moved to Arizona. Both of my parents got remarried. I was fortunate enough to gain three bonus siblings and instant best friends: my stepsister Shawna and my stepbrothers Curt and Johnny. My dad and stepmother had my baby brother Max. I mean, I had change just like any other person in the world. Most of it was good.

Then, in seventh grade, around my thirteenth birthday, I hit a wall. All teenagers go through lots of changes during this time. Teenage change is nothing out of the ordinary, but for me it was more than just teenage hormones and emotions raging through my veins. I was dealing with my mental illness on top of all of that.

Once again, my state of existence was not functional. I could not stop crying. It was the only thing I could do to respond to the empty feeling. It reminded me much of the overwhelming panic that I experienced in third grade, only now I was much older. Problems were bigger. Getting out of bed in the morning was nearly impossible, and from the moment I woke up, the dark feeling of sadness crept in and the only thing I could do is cry. That is what I did all the way to the bus, into the school, during homeroom, and to the guidance counselor's office.

This was the first time that I recall the morbid thoughts of suicide creeping into my head. I knew that I would not follow through on the thoughts, but they still were there in my mind daily as I dealt with the pain and anguish my depression caused.

I was young and not emotionally mature enough to comprehend my mental illness. I was getting good grades, I had many friends, I wasn't picked on at school, I made the traveling basketball team that I loved being on, and I had the clothes and teenage things I desired coming from a middle-class, white, privileged family.

And yet, I was miserable. Try explaining that.

It just goes to show you how the mind is the most powerful organ of the human body. The mind starts to go, and the rest of a person's existence follows. My depression was telling me negative things that weren't true. Sure, at first I could take a step back and realize the ridiculousness of what my illness was telling me, but there is only so long that a person can fight off mental illness. Eventually fighting off the thoughts was a full-time job. Untreated, my mental illness would eventually take over my mind, body, and soul. The illness would take over, sending an ache to every muscle, limb, and bone. It even got to the point where I was convinced my fingernails and hair hurt.

In seventh grade, I would spend a good portion of my school days at the guidance counselor crying. If it were a better day, I would somehow manage to pull myself back to class. The guidance counselor was not comforting in any way. She was not good at hiding the fact that she had no idea what to do with me. That made me feel like I was a lost cause or a freak. She always wanted answers to what happened. I had nothing to give her. She wanted to know if I was getting bad grades, if I was having issues with friends, or if things were bad at home. I had lots of friends, I was getting good grades, I was on the traveling basketball team, and nothing was happening at home. I could not give her the reason that made sense to her.

I lost my appetite. I could not sleep unless it was out of pure exhaustion. I would go to basketball practice and have a crying spell as I put on my shoes. I am not sure how long this lasted before my mother took me to see a doctor. It seemed like forever, but it was probably a couple weeks. A day during a depressive episode could seem like an eternity. Every day the sorrow seemed to consume me more, and I just began to live my life in this awful place.

On top of everything else, I felt alone. Isolation is not a healthy place to be trapped in when going through depression. This is part of what everyone goes through in their teenage years, but with mental health issues it was all the more complicated. I did not have anyone to talk to about it who I felt understood. I did not know anyone else who was going through this horrific situation, let alone someone my age. I felt like an alien on planet Earth. It was not as though I believed that I was really the only teenager in the world who had ever gone through this, but I had not been exposed to anyone else who had. The adults who worked with me always seemed baffled about what to do with me when I told them what I was going through. How was anyone able to help me break through this if they had no understanding of what I was going through? I was a walking contradiction. Everything in my life looked good on paper, but I was absolutely miserable.

Once my mother took me to our family doctor, they decided to put me on medication immediately. There were side effects. The drug made my stomach hurt, and I had less of an appetite and nausea, but these were nothing compared to the actual depression. The medication made me functional again. I met with all my teachers to explain what was going on with me so they could help me keep my grades up if there were any issues. They were all very understanding.

I don't recall much of the doctor's visit, but I do remember that the thought was I had some form of depression. Mental illness is difficult to comprehend because everyone experiences it differently. In the case of depression, the biochemical makeup of a person's brain is disrupted. In other words, my brain was not programmed the same way as most people's.

I discovered a way to understand and explain what my depression was like as a child. I remember it came to me as I sat patiently in the waiting room for my therapist. I watched a little kid in blue overalls and blonde pigtails struggling to hammer a rectangular peg into a round hole. I compared my depression to the children's game because it was a perfect example of the receptors in my brain not firing correctly. More specifically, the neurotransmitters serotonin, norepinephrine, and dopamine are the typical problem areas for people with depression. The receptors between neurons in my brain did not match, causing the imbalance in my brain chemistry. The peg was square and needed to be round.

The fact that I had more of an understanding of what was happening to me brought me some form of comfort. The unknown future did not. I continued to take my medication every day, and every day I felt a little bit better. After about seven or eight months, the doctor said I could gradually come off it completely. I was back to my usual self, and life continued as it had before.

Being a teenager at the time, I did not look back much once I was better. My focus was not on my mental health once I felt like myself again. I quickly jumped into the routines of hanging out with friends, crushing on boys, going to basketball practice, and playing games. The doctors were unsure if anything would happen again. We were told to come back if we noticed any signs of my moods going down this similar path. In my teenage mindset, I felt that the worst was behind me. Why worry about something that might not happen again.

Chapter Eight

JOURNAL ENTRY, AGE THIRTEEN

I had a dream. I am in a hospital gown. I feel the cold cement floor on my feet as my back rests against the back wall of the prison cell I find myself in. I hug my knees as a form of comfort and way to stay warm. I am in a dark room. The only connection to the outside world is a tiny ray of light that spotlights the floor in front of me. It's streaming in from the irregularly small square panel window on the door. I don't panic or question why I am there. I know it's my mental illness. In fact, I have visited this prison cell image in my mind before. I don't stir or fidget. I am stone. The numbness in my body has been that way for days and the only thing I can do to find any relief is let the tears stream. My eyes, that are typically soulful and taking in as much of the world's beauty as possible, are glazed over. I know this because I find it more and more difficult to even imagine anything outside that ray of light. That ray of light is the only thing that is keeping me teth- ered to reality. I curl up by this ray of light. I put my hand out and let it rest there. For a moment it brings me a small speck of joy. I focus on this tiny ray of light as if my life depended on it. I hold that ray of light in the palm of my hand because it gives me some sense of hope. I know for certain if I let it go, I would disappear into myself and fall into darkness.

Chapter Nine

THE WELL

Nick and I were not even halfway to Black River Falls. I sat, eyes glazed over, staring out the window and only thinking about Grandma Ellen. I pictured her looking down on me in complete disappointment. I was more ashamed of myself than I had ever been. I was enraged with myself.

What in the hell was I doing to myself? Had I not learned anything?

I was, at that time, in my early twenties, and I still had not fully accepted the fact that I had a mental illness. I still had not grasped onto the reality that I would be dealing with my depression for my entire life. It was not just going to go away.

I had to stop the denial. I was kidding myself.

Mental illness is not just cured.

It can only be treated. In my case, it can only be treated with medication and hard work in taking care of myself.

I had to be honest that I had not been taking care of myself.

Sitting in the passenger seat in silence, watching the farmland outside my window, I felt that I was lingering un-willingly out on the edge of insanity. Darkness and evil were starting to take over my every thought. I was witnessing how mental illness left untreated could overtake any human being's mind if presented the correct circumstance.

This is how good people turn evil or fall into darkness. I understood that if I did not take care of myself, I would inevitably be consumed by the darkness completely. Without taking care of myself, I would be lost. My illness would take over. I would find death or simply be a passenger in my own body.

So, with each breath, I allowed my body and mind to completely surrender to the darkness that existed inside me. I fell further and further inside of my body. A well growing deeper and deeper from the light of day. This daylight embodied my true form, and I watched it as it continued to grow smaller and smaller, trapping me inside my case of body, revealing to me that my true form soon would only be the watcher.

I had to pinch myself to shake myself back to reality. I found Nick looking at me with his usual smile. I half smiled back, thinking to myself that he was an oblivious, lucky bastard and how I would pay money to be that unaware of where I had just gone. I knew that I appeared silent and still, but inside it was as if I had just seen a horror movie that had shaken me to the core. Depression is like watching a movie. Specifically, a horror flick. Only long after the killer has jumped out of the closet with an ax and the lights come back on, you still feel terror.

Picture walking into a movie theater, popcorn crunching from numerous audience members, the red velvet curtain outlining the screen, the buttery smell in the air. You move through the aisles searching for familiar faces but find none. You weave your way to a seat near the middle, clutching your oversized Diet Coke and settle in, excited see the flick. Then it hits you that you don't even know what movie you are seeing, and before you can ask one of the strangers sitting near you, the lights dim and background chatter fades.

Expecting to see previews or the usual ad with dancing concessions, you drop your Diet Coke when you see your name flash across the screen, followed by your picture and your story. The shiver of iced soda seeps into your sock and shoes, but you can't take your eyes off the screen because you are watching your own life story unfold right before your eyes, without your control. Without you being present in your own life.

Mental illness is genetically woven into a person's brain chemistry like a piece of yarn in an afghan blanket. Removing that piece of yarn ultimately leaves the blanket full of holes, tattered and falling apart. If I did not take my illness seriously and work hard to treat it, I would inevitably fall apart.

At that moment, I took a deep breath in and allowed

myself to let what I was feeling flow through me. I wanted to remember the feeling that I felt right there at that moment in the car. The feeling that there was a basement to rock bottom and I was living in it. I wanted to be able to pause that horrible moment and plant it in my mind. Hell, if I could have frozen that moment in time, I would have blown it up, framed it, and put it above my mantle to guarantee that I'd never forget it.

Instead, I did the next best thing. I promised myself right there and then, somewhere between La Crosse and Black River Falls, that I would never forget how terrified I was at that moment. I was screaming inside, and that was exactly what I wanted to remember every time I thought about not taking my medication. I left the bottom of that well that day, and to this day I look back on that moment as a reminder of why I will never stop taking my medication again.

Chapter Ten

THE KID

The state track-and-field meet took place yearly at the National Sports Center in Blaine after the regular high school track-and-field season. Every runner had to qualify in each event by winning the event in regions or by running in under a particular time. All the fastest runners in the state of Minnesota compete. It was a difficult meet to qualify for and an honor to attend.

I was a scrawny little ninth grader with a mouth full of metal glistening in the sun. That year, I was the only female runner and person in my grade to qualify for the state track meet, and it was for the 400-meter dash. I knew of many of the older boys who were going to state, but I did not know any of them personally. I suppose it did not help that I was still at the junior high school.

All my girlfriends were jealous—not jealous of my making it to the state track and field meet but jealous that I got to train with and meet all the cutest boys in high school. I could not disagree with my friends for thinking that this group of older guys was hot, because they were. Unfortunately, some of the guys were not afraid to sit and tell you how awesome they were. Not exactly my type of fun. It did not really matter much anyway, as I had worked hard to qualify for the state meet and was focused on doing well.

I could not help but think of my grandma Ellen on that first day of state practice. At that moment I felt closer to her than I ever had before. I remember thinking this is what she must have felt like back when she was the only female who qualified and played in the naval air station golf tournament. Only that was in 1949, so I am sure she had to deal with much more than I did. For example, I know that many men dropped out because they did not want to play against a girl in a golf match. Or, as my grandpa said, they just did not want to lose to a girl. My grandma ended up in a sudden-death match with a man, and she ended up winning the entire tournament.

I kept the thought close to my heart as I prepared for the first day of practice. I had to leave my classes early at the junior high so my coach could drive me to the high school. I was mortified as her hunk-of-junk full-size van pulled up in front of the high school track. You could hear the van long before it came into view. The noticeable sound was a mixture of an absent muffler and a vehicle being driven long after its retirement age. The noise was so distracting that you couldn't help but turn and look.

To make matters worse, all the boys were already on the

track stretching as my trusty ride pulled up. I had to push all my weight on the door with my shoulder to get it to open. It made an earsplitting metal-on-metal sound as I got out. I thought, *I could not have made a grander entrance to the practice.* Then I thought of my grandma and what she must have gone up against. I pictured men yelling at her to go back to her place in the kitchen or assuming she was a lesbian because she was athletic and powerful. Who cares if she was female? What about common human decency? If she could keep going back then, well, I certainly owed it to myself and to her to continue onward. So I did. I took a deep breath and started by placing one foot in front of the other. With my face burning with redness, I joined my teammates in the circle of the field.

Coach Bear, who had already taken me under his wing through the season, gave me a nod as I arrived and yelled, "Hey, kid!" To this day I still haven't figured out if he called me that because I was so young or because he just could not remember my name, but it stuck for the rest of my varsity track career.

As I walked toward the circle of gorgeous older guys, all eyes were on me, and I could feel my face growing hot and red. I despised having the focus on me in general. In this case, I owed a big thanks to the sound of my arrival in the junker van. As I joined the rest of the team, all I could think about was whether I had anything stuck in my braces. Until that moment, I had not realized that a moment could be both wonderful and embarrassing at the same time.

Coach Bear lived up to his name, as he was the size of a linebacker. This was appropriate, as he was also head coach of Burnsville's varsity football team. He wore short gym-teacher shorts with striped knee socks along with his sneakers. A mustache—which he was constantly touching, as if he needed reassurance that it still was there—outlined the line of his lip. He had the coaching strategy of an army drill sergeant. He spit when he talked. Everyone really valued having him as a coach, and they listened. I sure did. You wanted to make him proud. He had a way of bringing the best athlete out of people.

Coach Bear twisted his mustache and waited for us all to settle down before he opened practice.

"For those of you who don't know, this is Kris Berg. The lone female ninth grader going to state this year with us in the four-hundred-meter dash. Please welcome her and show her the ropes on this magnificent experience. I expect you to all be gentlemen to her. It's more than likely she will pass some of you on the track because she is faster than you. All right, two laps warm up, ladies and gentlemen, and let's get back over here for stretching. No slacking or we all do two more."

All the boys immediately started jogging and chattering

with one another before I could finish removing my warm-ups. I had just started to jog to catch up with the rest of the team when a blue-eyed, blond-haired boy entered the track and headed toward me.

"Hi, care if I warm up with you?"

"Not at all," I said as we started running side by side.

"I'm Matt Pelant. Don't worry about them. If they aren't kissing their biceps after school in the weight room, they are telling you how awesome their biceps are."

"Kris, Kris Berg," I said.

And just like that, my nervousness vanished, and Matt Pelant entered my life. We started jogging side by side on the track, chatting. We had something in common, as he was the only sophomore who made the state team. He was an alternate in the four-by-four that usually won state. He was feeling the pressure, as they had a legacy to uphold and it sounded like he would be running because one of their seniors did not care to run due to all the graduation events. I thought he was lucky to have the opportunity. I had seen him run before, and he was a contender.

"Why did Coach Bear have to tell all the guys that I could possibly run faster than them?" I asked Matt.

"Well, first, we all have seen you beat many guys in practice this season." He laughed. "And second, he wants to motivate us all."

"I see his point," I said. "At this rate, I will be one of the fastest girls in the state of Minnesota but won't be able to find a prom date."

By that time, we had run our warm-ups and started heading to the circle to stretch with the rest of the guys. Matt looked at me, smirking.

"What is so funny?" I asked him.

"Nothing," Matt said, laughing. "It's just that, if I had to guess, you aren't the type of girl who would care if a guy was intimidated by your athletic abilities."

"Yeah, I guess you are right," I said. "I wouldn't want to date someone who had a problem with it anyway."

As we stretched, we all goofed around and chatted. Suddenly I was laughing and talking with everyone.

Once we got through most of our stretching routine, Coach Bear stood up to announce the plan for practice that day.

"Okay, we are going to work on starts for the rest of practice. We want to make sure you get out of those blocks right. It can make the difference in winning or being disqualified. You all know at state there are no second chances if you jump the gun. I will be using the actual start gun to help you prepare. Make sure you put your spikes on as well. There is no messing around here, people. Act like this is the real deal. Finish up your stretches, get your spikes, and then meet me at the hundred-meter starting line in five minutes."

With that, everyone scattered one by one after finishing up their stretches. They all headed to the hundred-meter dash starting line but stopped to grab their spikes and some water on the way over.

I decided to take my time. I did not want to be the first person out of the blocks. I wanted to step back and learn from the rest of the team members, who were more experienced than I was. Then one of the seniors, Tyrone Hanson, started heading toward me. Everyone knew of Tyrone Hanson. He was the star football player. He had that smooth black skin and an athletic build, not to mention washboard abs. Most girls would swoon as he walked by. The fact that I got to practice with Tyrone made all my friends jealous. Why was he headed toward me? My first instinct was to see if anyone was behind me, even though I knew nobody was. He was right in front of me, and I knew my face was turning red.

"Hi, Kris," Tyrone said.

"Hi, Tyrone," I said, knowing I looked shocked. He knew my name. He knew my name.

"Your mom is the one who is a legend around here for cheering, right? Everyone clears away from her in the stands because she is so loud?"

"Yup, that's my mom," I said, laughing.

At all my meets, I could find her easily. She was kind of a legend on my team.

"Some of the others mentioned that she cheers for lots of your teammates, and I was wondering, since my parents can't come to state, could you ask if she will cheer for me?" Tyrone said this looking kind of embarrassed.

"Of course," I said. "And you'll be able to hear her at state from the blocks as well."

"Thanks, Kris. I owe you," he said, and with that he jogged off to grab his spikes and join everyone else who had already made way down to the starting line.

Once I knew nobody was around, I did a little self-cheer. I could not wait to tell my friends about that moment. They were going to die.

I ran by my sports bag, flung my tied-together spikes over my shoulder, and headed to join the rest of the team before Coach Bear. I knew I had a big, stupid, metal grin on my face at that moment. I did not care. I was right where I was supposed to be, and I could feel Grandma Ellen by my side cheering me on. Not only had I met Matt that day. The big man on campus came to talk to me. Me of all people. I felt accepted by them all and now there was only one thing left to do, and that was run fast. I knew I could do that.

Chapter Eleven

THE LONGEST WALK
IN MINNESOTA

Finally, it was prelims of for the state meet, or what my coach called *the dance*. This was my first time at the state track-and-field meet. I could feel my nervousness in every inch of my body. I mean, even my hair and fingernails ached with anticipation. I had made it this far. What would be my next chapter?

Once again, I felt the strength of my grandma Ellen with me. Perhaps this nervousness was what she felt as she set down her golf clubs on the green and prepared to tee off from her first hole that day in 1949 when she won the naval air station golf tournament? I wondered if she had a routine to calm her nerves. Was she superstitious? For example, I always had to put my right spike on before my left spike before a race. I remember once, in an attempt to break my one ritual, I tried to put my left shoe on first. I could not do it. It just didn't feel right. I had to take off my shoes and start all over again. It might sound silly, but if putting on my shoes a certain way made me feel better going into my race, hey, I'd take it. The way I saw it, I was fortunate to not have any extreme superstitions or routines like some of my fellow athletes.

I was finishing up my warm-up, which consisted of standard stretches and interval sprints. My arms were over-dramatically moving as they pushed and pulled, assisting my movement over the track. I focused on the zipping sound of my warm-ups rubbing against each other to keep myself distracted from my nerves. Usually by the time I warmed up for a track race, my nerves would die down.

Not today.

Today was different.

On this day, I was warming up for the meet that I had prepared for all season. I thought about all the miles I had run, the numerous sprint drills, and the times I'd practiced my start out of the blocks over the season. I was ready, and no stupid superstition or luck had brought me to that moment. I had brought myself to that moment with hard work. Even if this rush of nervousness continued until the gun went off for my race, I was as ready as I could be. Now all I could do was run. That was all I had to do. What was the worst that could happen anyway, I run around in a little circle slower than the rest of my competitors? I smiled, thinking about how all the hype was about running around in a circle as fast as I could go. When I thought about how absurd it sounded, suddenly it didn't seem so intimidating anymore. I could take a deep breath and relax.

I sat on the floor of the indoor track with my headphones on. Suddenly I looked up to see Matt Pelant and a few of the other guys trying to say something. My music was blasting, so I could only see their mouths moving. I motioned to my headphones as I quickly took them off.

"Good luck, Kris," Matt said with the guys behind him repeating his words.

"Thanks, you guys. I am so nervous that I feel light-headed," I said.

"You'll do great. Just wanted to quick stop by before your event and wish you well," Matt said.

"I appreciate it, you guys," I said.

"We will be all out there cheering for you," he said.

"Well, you have to cheer louder than my mom," I said.

The group all laughed and muttered, "Yeah, right."

With that, the group walked away and started to head outside to the track. Part of me wished that I were joining them all to watch from the bleachers. The nerves were overtaking my body again. I was just about to put my headphones back on when I heard over the intercom,

"Girls AA four-hundred-meter dash prelims, please check in."

There was a brief pause, and then the announcer repeated the words once more.

"Girls AA four-hundred-meter dash prelims, please check in."

I could hear the microphone being set down, and the clunk of it echoed off the walls of the indoor facility until it faded into the distance.

The reality sunk in. It would soon be my time to march out of the tunnel and onto the track for my event. I had been nervous since I woke up that morning, but this was an entirely new level of nervousness. It was an uneasiness that made my face completely go numb, my ears ring, and my stomach feel like I was about to be reunited with the energy bar that I ate earlier. Nobody, especially me, wanted that. Those were nasty enough going down.

I laughed to myself as I flashed back to my friend Justin shoving an entire peanut butter energy bar in his mouth on a dare and chewing until it was completely gone. Justin won that dare, and it really was legendary. I remember the entire team was camped out behind the bleachers cheering him on with every bite, and when it was gone he bowed. The energy bars had been with me since my first meet, and they were reliable. It was not a superstition. It's what I could eat that wouldn't upset my stomach before a meet. It was funny to think about how that energy bar had been my trusty sidekick for that year of meets, and that was more than I could say about some of the people I'd crossed paths with in life.

I shook my head back and forth in an attempt to get out of my daydreaming head and focus on the present. My event would be soon. I ran in place as fast as I could while focusing on my breathing to get myself grounded. I tended to hold my breath when I was nervous.

I checked in with the lady who clenched the clipboard of names as if her life depended on it. The tension she projected was so thick that I could have done the backstroke through it. When it was my turn, I gave her my name. I tried to not let her shortness affect me as I watched her put a check mark next to my name, confirming I was in lane six. Lane six was not the lane I wanted to be in—the best lanes were four or five—but I was just proud that I was in prelims at the state meet. I lined up with the others in numerical order. I looked around to see all the familiar faces I had run against all season.

The lady let go of her extended limb of a clipboard just long enough to hand out the lane number stickers to everyone. Without hesitation, I pulled down my warm-up pants and stuck it to the right thigh of my track shorts. I knew most of the runners around me, but it was a mutual understanding that nobody talked before a big race. None of us even made eye contact, almost like we were in fear of losing focus or taking on our competitors' nerves. The solo sound of the movement of warm-up pants zipped through the air as we all fidgeted, stretched, and moved to keep our muscles warm. I put my headphones back on to help distract myself from the nerves. Music had a way of motivating me.

I knew what lay ahead of us as we entered the stadium. The guys had warned me about the local media. There was a tunnel lined with reporters yelling our names and flashing their cameras, attempting to get that great picture or quote. Even small local media had a way of being invasive at the worst possible moment.

Finally, the clipboard lady gave us the okay to start lining up and moving toward the tunnel. I turned up the volume of my Walkman radio. Yes, that is correct: it was the yellow sports Walkman radio. No, we did not have iPods yet. The closest thing to that was an MP3 player, and I did not own one. So I rocked the Walkman radio.

"Ramble On" by Led Zeppelin blasted through my headphones, pumping adrenaline through my veins. That song just got me moving, and it was my personal attempt to drown out the outside world. I had to picture myself ahead of my competitors and could not let the local media distract my focus. I knew it was much too easy to slip and let the nerves take over sending me down a negative spiral. I had to stay strong mentally, visualize my run, and be completely present in my body as it took motion. The littlest of distractions could pull an athlete out of their rhythm.

All of us female 400-meter runners headed on our path to the stadium. To this day I still think of this moment as the longest walk in Minnesota. In reality, the distance was not very far, but to me it felt like an eternity. I knew that I was about to run against the fastest 400-meter runners in the state. I was going out to represent Burnsville High School. It was what I worked for all season. It was my time to take in the music and enjoy the moment. I earned it.

Again, I thought of my grandma Ellen. I pictured her joining the first female class in the Navy, the Women Accepted for Volunteer Emergency Service (WAVES), established when President Franklin D. Roosevelt signed the Navy Women's Reserve Act on July 30, 1942. I pictured her playing on the winning basketball team, hitting a softball, and wearing her mechanic jumpsuit while she worked on the Navy planes. If she could do all these things during a time where women were expected mostly to be housewives, I could easily do this.

As I imagined my grandma Ellen go through all these impressive events, I forgot about my nerves once more. I felt that her accomplishments had somehow empowered me to be where I was at that moment. I recall feeling so aware of each step, each breath as if everything went by in slow motion. It was as if time were at a standstill, just like a scene out of a movie. I convinced myself that the flashes coming from either side of the tunnel leading to the stadium were flashes of light moving with the music to keep myself calm. I was never a fan of big crowds or being the center of attention. In fact, I could not wait to get inside the entrance of the stadium to hide from the cameras, even if it were only for a moment.

Once I got there, I held onto every breath and blink of eye in an attempt to delay the inevitable crowd and event that existed on the other side. I knew that stadium was full and thousands of eyes and college recruiters would soon be watching my every move. I would not let my head go to that place. So I did what I trained myself to do: I suddenly stopped my mind from spiraling out of control by focusing on all the hours of preparation I put into this track season.

My mind flashed back to the miles, practices, and dedication I put into this. Soon I was calmer, and the nerves diminished. I tried to grasp onto that calm blanket of confidence before it departed like a shooting star in the night sky. So I had to focus on the music. I could see up ahead the edge of the tunnel that led to the stadium.

All runners lined the edge of the tunnel, peering into the stadium. In my head, every seat was filled, even if that were not the case. We settled there just in time to hear the gun go off for the event before ours. The loud sound made some of my competitors jump and snapped me out of my happy musical world and right back into reality. Then we heard it. Something no track runner wants to hear. The sound of a second gun going off. Instantly, the invisible walls between all my competitors vanished. We all looked at each other gasping in shock. Oh no! The crowd even silenced. We knew the sound of a second gun meant one of two things. A false start or some technical error in the process.

"Please be an error, please be an error," I said out loud.

I scanned the area to see my competitors' mouths agape and headphones off, waiting to hear what was going on. If it was a false start, it meant disqualification to a runner. To make it all this way to the state prelims and then be disqualified was completely horrifying. We all continued to chat and glance back and forth at each other, collectively wanting the outcome to be technical. The disappointment of the crowd said it all as we watched as one of the fastest girls in the state of Minnesota in the hundred-meter dash be disqualified.

She jumped the gun. This is not something that even her closest competitor would wish for. The crowd was booing and screaming their disapproval. We all watched in horror as the race went on without hesitation or sympathy. Disqualification was a runner's greatest fear, and we knew that all it took was an eager sleight of foot out of the blocks for any of us to be in her shoes. It made me feel frustrated to think that nobody would ever truly know who would have won the race because not all qualifiers participated. They should have given her another chance, for the sake of the entire event.

Despite experiencing a negative outcome, it brought all the girls running my event to an even foundation of mutual respect. After all, we were all in this together, and it was comforting to know that we all were going through similar nervousness. I shook my arms and legs out as I came back to Earth.

"And now the Minnesota girls AA four-hundred-meter dash prelims," the announcer stated over the stadium amplifiers.

That was our cue to line up in our lane and jog to our starting block as they announced our names over the stadium intercom.

"Lane six: Kris Berg from Burnsville, Minnesota."

I could hear my mother cheering long before I spotted her in the crowd next to the rest of my family. I turned to wave to them, and I could see my mother jumping up and down screaming my name.

The laughter brought on by my mother's cheering made me start to lighten up. Really, in this situation, what is the worst thing that could happen? I could fall on my face. At least that would be funny. I was just running, and I did it because I enjoyed it. It gave me comfort to really step back and realistically view the situation.

I set up my blocks precisely and practiced a few starts as I warmed up my legs. My starts had really come a long way this year. Once I felt ready to go, I put my warm-ups away in the basket sitting behind my blocks. I was so focused that I did not realize at first there was a girl sitting on a box marked lane six ready to hold my blocks and take my warm-ups to the finish line for me. I felt so important. It was as if I had an assistant. I wondered if she would take my drink order too. I stood in front of my blocks without moving to show the announcer I was ready to go.

Eventually, all the runners were standing at attention in front of their blocks, waiting for those words. The entire stadium grew silent.

"Runners, take your mark . . ."

I scurried into my blocks, lined my fingers perfectly along my lane start line. I recall pulling out a wedgie to ensure I was completely comfortable before I showed ready stillness.

"Set . . ."

I pushed my butt straight up in the air, focused my weight, and—

Bang!

The gun went off, and I shot out of the blocks just like

Coach Bear taught me to. My nerves were high, and I was too much in my head. The best races I had were the ones I did not remember anything from the gun to crossing the finish line.

This race was not one of my best or most focused. I remember every detail along the way. I could hear the crowd. I kept thinking about how my coach warned me that, unlike the pill-shaped track I usually ran on, this track was a circle. Typically, I put in everything I had when I came across the last curve, but this time, I would not have that warning before the end. The finish line would come up on me much faster than I expected.

That is exactly what happened to me this time. I did not use all my energy in my tank and, before I knew it, I was crossing the finish line. I was not last in my heat or anything, but it was not my best performance. I did not advance to the finals that took place the next day.

I was a little disappointed that I did not do better, but I could not be upset after making it as far as I did. I was just proud that I survived my first state meet. Next year, I would be prepared. After all, I still had three more years of high school track to get better.

Chapter Twelve

WHISPERS

Back on the winding roads of Wisconsin, Nick was drumming on the steering wheel as the song "Black Dog" by Led Zeppelin came over the radio. I chose to turn my face toward the breeze coming in from the open window and focus on anything that could help me through the eternity it was taking us to get to the hospital. I started to look through the photo album of memories in my mind.

It was three days after Christmas my sophomore year of high school when the event happened under the Cedar Avenue Bridge. I had been hanging out with my girlfriends that night, and we had just picked up our friend Krista. We had been catching up on what happened over her holiday on the drive to our destination when Krista blurted out, "Matt Pelant died."

I immediately felt all the blood rush to my head.

"Wait, what are you talking about?" I said.

Krista said it again coldly. "I guess some guy named Matt Pelant killed himself last night. He took a shotgun to his head in his truck. The police said they got an anonymous call to go check down by the river under the Cedar Avenue

Bridge. They think he was the one who called so they would find him right away. My sister, who was in the high school leadership group with him, just told me she got a call right before I left."

I must have looked like I was going to puke, and I could see it on Krista's face that she just understood that I knew him. At that moment, I could picture Matt driving his truck down under the Cedar Avenue Bridge, where high school kids drove to all the time to go look at the river or hang out with friends. Only now I was the one behind the wheel, crying, and my only company was the gun sitting in the passenger seat. I could feel the pain. I could feel the horrible pain of my depression as I continued to flash between myself and Matt Pelant as he and I put the shotgun toward our heads and heard the gun go off. Then I saw us both running in a meet.

I was not someone who drove around when I had an episode. I had never gone under the Cedar Avenue Bridge by myself or during an episode. I had seen a hunting rifle in my father's gun case, but I had never held one before. I had never gone through with the act of suicide, although I had lived with the secret of my suicidal thoughts for years. I didn't know Matt Pelant outside of the track-and-field team, but he went out of his way to be kind and make me feel welcome. At that moment, I realized there was someone who understood what I was going through. Only it was too late.

The flash of thoughts rushed through my mind, and I must have still looked like I was going to be sick. Krista put her hand on my shoulder, and it brought me back to my body.

"Oh my gosh, did you know him, Kris?" she said.

"Yes, I ran track with him," was all I could get out of my mouth.

"I'm so sorry, Kris. I didn't know him and had no idea you did. I would have been more sensitive in bringing it up," Krista said with a look of concern.

"It's okay, you didn't know. I didn't know him that well. I met him from track last year when I went to state. He was the guy who made me feel welcome. Can you please take me home?" I said, feeling like I was going to throw up.

"I guess he had been dealing with depression for years, and he had just started on a new medication that set him off. Anything we can do, Kris?" Krista said.

"No, but thank you. I just need to be by myself," I said.

I said goodbye to my friends as they pulled up in my driveway. I went straight to my room and closed the door. I am not sure how long I sat just processing in shock before I started crying. Time is not something that even comes to mind when trying to process such a horrific event.

I kept remembering his friendly face that first day of state track practice. He helped me fit in and feel welcome when

I really needed someone. I never thought in a million years that he was fighting off depression like me. He was the first other person I knew of who had depression. I was not alone with this. Only, I had no idea that he was depressed until he was gone.

He was gone.

He was gone.

Matt was gone.

The kind boy who helped me feel welcome at practice when I was uncomfortable and made feel part of the team. Matt with the great smile and sparkling blue eyes. Matt had taken a gun in a moment of his illness, driven his truck under the Cedar Avenue Bridge, and shot himself in the head. Matt was dead.

Matt was dead.

Matt was gone.

I could not grasp the reality of Matt being gone, even though I could understand the darkness of mental illness that led him to take his own life. Matt took his own life because he was sick, and that was how I saw it. I was quite familiar with the trail that brought him to the basement of rock bottom. Up until that point, I had not known of anyone else who had experienced depression like I had. I was not the only one who had a mental illness on top of teenage hormones and had thoughts of death constantly. So this was a big deal to me. I felt for the first time like someone my age was going through what I was. I was not alone.

But he was gone. It was too late.

The truth is, we don't talk about mental illness enough today. Back then, nobody did. Plus, we also did not understand mental illnesses like depression as well as we do now.

I was never angry at Matt for what he did. That is a natural reaction for people, and it is valid to feel that way. I just knew that it was beyond his control. I had been to the darkness off and on throughout my life. I had suicidal thoughts when I was in the thick of it. I believed that it was his illness that created his unfortunate passing. I understood he was not himself or in the right frame of mind when he pulled the trigger. I had been to numerous dark corners of my mind and lost control. Everyone does in life at some degree, but when you have a mental illness, it takes over the wheel while you sit in horror in the passenger seat.

I never felt his death was anyone's fault. I knew better. I knew from personal experience that all I ever wanted when I was at the end of my rope was for the excruciating pain to stop. That was it. That was all I could see. How could I blame him for wanting the same thing that I had wanted before? Matt's death happened because he was mentally ill.

There was this part of me that was angry at myself. Angry at myself for not speaking up about my own experiences.

Why is mental illness so stigmatized? Why do we isolate and keep the story limited to whispers left behind closed doors?

Why?

Why?

Why?

I was angry at myself. I wish I had opened up to him more. Maybe if I did, I could have helped. Maybe he would still be alive.

Maybe.

What if?

Why?

I was angry at myself and the mess of a system that failed him. I knew that the reality was there was nothing to be done. It was not anyone's fault. That is the tricky part about mental illness. When someone takes their own life, people want answers. They want to place blame. But it's an illness. Matt was sick and not in his right mind. He wasn't himself at the time. I was so angry at myself and ashamed that I had not told a single one of my friends what was going on with my depression at that moment. Something needed to change, but what?

Chapter Thirteen

BLUE

I have never thought of blue as a sad color. Blue shades are a breath of clean, pure, cool air in and out of your lungs. Blue is the color of sky on a summer day when you can't spot a cloud. Blue is the color that covers most of the earth's surface. It is the water that you pour into your plants and gardens, bringing forth energy and life. Blue is the water that we can see clear straight down to the sand-covered bottom as we decide to take a running start off the end of the dock and cannon ball into the cool refreshing water. It is the color of translucent waves as the aqua water crashes on the shores and sandy beaches of Secret Harbour in St. Thomas. Blue is the raindrops that fall in spring and wash all the death away, bringing new life to the earth. Blue is the snow and ice, a numbing grayish blue that you ice skate on when the lake freezes over, or the hills you ski on when the snow begins to fall. It is the color of compassion and relaxation, the color of music, when you feel like heading to Chicago or Milwaukee to listen to some good guitar riffs. Blues music is alive, raw, and emotional. Blue is a color that lets you know everything is going to be all right, the color I see after I have made it through a difficult situation or after I have made it out of a depressive episode. Blue brings that feeling of relaxation, a feeling you have when things are balanced once more.

Chapter Fourteen

BLACK RIVER FALLS

The black Subaru Impreza finally pulled up to Black River Falls Hospital. I was able to feel a moment of relief when we arrived in the hospital waiting room to find my dad waiting for us. My father had driven down from Minneapolis to meet us. As I approached, he gave me his all-too-familiar look of understanding where no words were needed. I gave him a huge hug and part of me felt like a child in pigtails as he scared away the monsters under my bed. Only I was not a child anymore and had not been for years. I was an adult in my early twenties, and the monsters were not under my bed but inside my head.

I was paralyzed as we sat in the waiting room. I had not had a good night of rest for days. I had not been able to eat. It was too much effort to hold small-talk conversations, but at the same time resting with my thoughts was like watching flashes of a horror flick that had no plot. The only thing that allowed me to feel some form of relief was movement. Movement helped me calm my insanity. It helped my mental illness settle into reality rather than unrealistic horrors and death.

So there I sat, staring at the linoleum floor, bouncing my leg up and down like a nervous twitch. As I focused on the movement of my leg to distract myself, I started to imagine myself back home running on the trails of Minnesota during my favorite season of fall. Suddenly in my mind I was there. It was flashes at first, but then my mind carried me to my memory in full. I felt my feet hitting the pavement and crunching the fall leaves. I could feel the fresh cool air in my lungs as I breathed it in and out, fueling my every limb. It was my body movement silencing my mind into some song of meditation. Then in the blink of an eye, my daydream was lost, and I was back to the waiting room, watching my leg rapidly move in utter disappointment, internalizing the question in my head that I had repeatedly gone over for days.

What the hell happened to me?

When and where did I make this decision to stop running? It was a healthy outlet that I enjoyed. I absolutely loved it, and I was good at it too. The two irritating words taunted me.

I was

I was

I was

I was an all-state track-and-field runner who was headed toward a scholarship to run in college. I was once someone who despised cigarettes and drinking. Now I was a barfly.

I was once someone who had been mindful of my overall well-being. I was once someone who believed in myself. I was a college graduate.

All I could see was someone who had given up, and that was not someone I was. I knew that part of me still existed but all that was left to show was the dried blood festering pus of a wound that was trying to heal, and I would not let it. I kept picking at it.

What the hell did I let happen to me?

My mind trailed off again in anger.

Suddenly the flashes of memories of me pulling out my pack of cigarettes at parties and as I hosted and ran the weekly open mic at a local blues bar. It does not take a genius to figure out running and smoking don't mix. That still did not stop my attempts to make it a possibility for the two habits to coexist.

In my early twenties, back in Minneapolis, it was my routine to run around Lake Calhoun, stretch at my car, and smoke a cigarette. I would get strange looks and double takes from people that I just ran by. I earned those nasty looks, but you could not tell me that back then. I was angry at the world, cast blame outside myself, and did not take responsibility for my own actions.

In the time it took to smoke one cigarette after a run, I would get at least two passive-aggressive people who would cough loudly, accompanied by a dramatic wave of the hand moving the smoke out of their face to let me know that I was not worthy of being near them. I was across the street from the bike and walking path. I was not intentionally blowing smoke in these poor people's faces. I got the look of hate from these strangers. They knew nothing about me besides the fact that I was a smoker, so naturally I had to be pure evil.

I understand not wanting to be by smoke, but then all I wanted was to have my moment of peace. I was angry that they had no comprehension of what I went through to allow myself to have that one cigarette. If they knew this was my only cigarette that day, would I be deemed worthy of a smile or hello? Would I be considered a fellow human being?

My mind wandered back to the waiting room, my leg moving up and down as the nurse stepped in and called my name. It was good timing. I wanted a cigarette and I had not had one in three months. The withdrawal was adding to my depression. I was determined to quit.

As I followed the nurse back through the maze of winding halls, everything seemed to slow down. I noticed every crack in the linoleum. Every passing face was judging me. The sound of a phone ringing as I passed the nurses' judging station had me jumping out of my skin. The nurses all stood there in the station laughing about something, but it felt as if they were all mocking me, the crazy girl.

I started to think about how I had been here before numerous times. Not at this exact hospital, but urgently seeking help for my depression. I had utilized all my energy over the past two weeks to fight off the negative thoughts and function as a typical human being. Exhaustion was taking over my mental clarity. I was starting to lose it.

I continued the circus charade march, following the nurse back to the examining room. The lights seemed to flicker on and off. At this point I accepted it was probably in my head. I had lost sense of what was real in my ill, tired state. More doctors passed, chatting and looking at files. I was almost terrified to look up because I knew I would make some story up in my head. I would picture them getting ready to lock me up in a straitjacket as I kicked and screamed and they threw me into a padded room, sedated by needle. The greatest fear in my life was losing my mind.

The sound of a nurse dropping her clipboard in front of me snapped me back to reality. In my mind, this walk through the hospital took an eternity, but really, I had only walked ten feet.

I knew without any doubt that if I didn't take my mental illness seriously from this point on, there wouldn't be a next time walking down a hall to a waiting room to talk to a family physician or psychiatrist for help. The only next time would be my dead body being wheeled down the hallway to the morgue.

I really took that moment to take in just how fortunate I was that over the years I had been able to get help before things got to the point of hurting myself, attempting suicide, or being locked up in the psych ward. This episode rattled fear to the core of my soul. I had never been so close to the edge of losing my mind and my will to live before. It was like being locked inside someone else's body. I had no control. I was afraid of myself and my thoughts. I was afraid for my life. I could not go through this again. I simply would not survive it.

I decided right there and then that this would be the last time that I played a role in contributing to my illness. I would take responsibility. Part of this was my fault. I should have stayed on my medication.

Finally, the nurse escorted me to a cold, sterile hospital room, where she sat me down to take my vitals. The nurse was about my age and round, with long, dark brown hair that was tied back in a ponytail. She introduced herself and put out her hand for me to shake. I recall this because it surprised me as an act that most nurses did not do. I put my hand in hers to return the friendly gesture. We talked as she took my vitals.

"Hi, it looks like you are here because you are having some issues with ongoing depression?" she said as she looked at the chart.

"Yes, I stopped taking my medication a little under two years ago or so because I thought I was better," I said. "I was completely fine for a while, and then out of nowhere I hit this wall."

"Can you explain what you mean by hitting a wall?" She gave me a profoundly serious look.

"I am not living. I'm simply existing and fighting to exist in a constant depressive state. I can't live this way," I said, tearing up.

The nurse smiled at me and said, "Well then, we will just have to find a way to help you today. The doctor will be in shortly."

Before she left the room, she handed me two awfully familiar forms to fill out. Because my depression was a recurring theme in my life, I would have to take the Patient Health Questionnaire 9 (PHQ-9) for depression, along with the Generalized Anxiety Disorder 7 (GAD-7) assessment. These surveys were a way to measure by a set scale how much I was struggling. I had taken them dozens of times before. In fact, to this day, even when I go for a basic checkup with my doctor, I must take them. I have come to appreciate the fact that my mental health is always on my doctors' radar even if it's not on mine. I filled it out meticulously and carefully because I wanted to be completely honest and accurate despite my urge to hold back.

After all that was complete, I still had to wait for the doctor to arrive. Realization kicked in that I was in the room all alone with nothing to distract me. No patient enjoys waiting in a little cell-like room when they are waiting to get a general checkup. Why did they make people coming in about mental illness wait so long? It was torture. At that time, I was the most vulnerable I had ever been. I was not stable. At that moment, being in that room alone, I may as well have been locked inside a padded room with the walls closing in on me.

Even the faded off-white colors in the room were making me feel anxious. What once appeared to be a crisp white wall aged into faded yellow complete with matching linoleum floors. I distinctly remember thinking that if the color had a name, it would be armpit stain. I was trapped. I was trapped in an armpit prison cell. I started to breathe shorter breaths in and out, causing my head to spin. If it had continued, I would have spiraled into one of my usual panic attacks, but the doctor entered the room, bringing my sick mind back to reality.

Surprisingly, this doctor looked to be the same age as me. I remember wondering if he had gone to medical school as a baby. It at least brought a smile to my face. He came in, introduced himself, and shook my hand. The handshake must have been a company protocol.

"Hi, Kris. I was able to get your files, and I see you have clinical depression. Looks like we need to put you back on your medication, and if it's okay, I'd also like to temporarily put you on some antianxiety pills to get you back on your feet."

"Yes, doctor. I don't plan to stop taking my medication ever again, even if I'm fine for three years after. This depression will always come back."

"You had luck with the last prescription you were on, correct?" he said, flipping through pages.

"Yes, I was put on medication senior year in high school that made me worse, numb to everything and suicidal. Then, after my freshman year of college, we tried a different prescription that made my mind race all over the place. It felt like my head would explode. Finally, I was put on a prescription that worked for me."

"Okay, can you go pick up the prescription right away?" he asked.

"Yes, my dad came to pick me up and bring me back home to Minneapolis for a long weekend. Once I get home, I will check in with my regular doctor as well. We can pick it up right away. The sooner, the better," I said.

"One more thing I need to ask you before you go is, do you feel that you will harm yourself? I can check you in here today if that is the case," he said with a serious look on his face.

"I will be fine. I know that once I start taking my medication, I will get better," I said.

The doctor stood up and shook my hand. "You will get better, but you have to continue to take your medication to stay balanced."

"Don't worry, there is no way I will let this happen again," I said.

Chapter Fifteen

THIRD IN STATE

The announcement came loudly over the intercom at my second state meet finals.

"Girls four-hundred-meter dash finals, please check in."

I had already done my warm-up routine and was stretching nearby on the indoor track in a meditative state when the loud disruptive noise continued on over the intercom.

"Girls four-hundred-meter dash finals, check in."

Like the previous year, I gathered my warm-ups and spikes as I headed over to check in. I couldn't shake the feeling that something was missing, so I turned back to make sure I didn't leave anything behind. It wasn't until I confirmed that I had everything that I realized I was asking the wrong question. It wasn't what I was missing but who was missing.

The spring, after Matt's death, track season came around again as if nothing had changed. Only it had changed. People graduated and moved on with their lives. Matt was gone. I was finishing up my sophomore year, the first year my classes were at the high school. The rusty old van was now just a memory and a running joke with the guys who witnessed it the previous season.

That year, I was not only at my fastest speed, but I was also experienced, and that made me confident. During that period, I had some of my personal best placements in the state of Minnesota for track and field. I won conferences and regionals in the four-hundred-meter dash, leading me to qualify for state again.

Lisa Mickelson, a girl I knew from basketball, started running the four hundred that year. She was a year older than me and could run at my speed. Not only were we able to challenge each other to become faster runners, but we also ended up being close friends. We supported each other without bringing nastiness into our competitive world. So many females have a tendency to take their closest competitors as a threat and aren't able to become friends. It's unfortunate to make competitive rivals enemies, because not only do you miss out on a possible friendship, but you also miss out on having a relationship with the one person who can push you to improve your craft the most. I was fortunate to have a friend like Lisa challenge me and support me at the same time. It's a rare thing with teenage girls.

My first year of high school was positive. I had already made friends with some of the upperclassmen from track before I arrived. I had finally started to find a group of friends that I trusted and could confide in. I was playing varsity basketball and running track.

Still, through all the success and happiness, I could not shake off the loss of our teammate Matt. The thought that it could have just as easily been me lingered in the back of my head.

Matt should have been there with us. How was it that life and track practice could continue to move forward so easily while he has ceased to exist? I had to admit it made me appreciate what I had, although at the same time I felt guilty. Matt's ashes were in a lockbox representing his tombstone in the cemetery next door to the high school while we were all warming up for track practice.

The Pelant family donated the team pole-vaulting equipment in Matt's honor. I knew he'd pole-vaulted, but I didn't realize how much he'd valued it until the equipment arrived and the coaches told us about it at practice one day. Most of the team saw the equipment as a memorial for Matt and found comfort in seeing it every day at practice.

I did not find comfort in seeing this equipment at all. Much like I didn't, and still don't, find comfort when going to a funeral or visiting a gravestone. Many people do find comfort in this, and I am envious of these people. I wish that I could feel that way. I don't have it in me. I don't feel like I'm visiting the dead as I walk to a tombstone. I feel like I am visiting a slab of stone and dirt. My loved one is not there anymore. I feel my loved one's soul isn't tied to his body or grave; it is everywhere. A lost one's soul, to me, is tied to the people they loved and left behind. The soul is energy and to me that has to go somewhere. In my mind it is an unexplainable utopia. Then the question comes up well, what about hell? I don't believe it exists. Well, then where do horrible people go? I'd argue that horrible people don't have souls. My sister and I would call awful people "filler people." A filler person is someone that was born when God had no souls to give out. Therefore, a filler person is an empty shell. A horrible person simply ceases to exist.

Even though I knew Matt was gone, my mind couldn't grasp the reality of it. I would find myself scanning the track looking for him because I wanted to tell him something. Then I would remember he was gone and the knot in my stomach would tie tighter.

I needed to do something instead of just rest with these feelings and realizations. I personally had struggled with mental illness my entire life, and I owed it to Matt to talk about my own experiences.

So that is what I did.

If more people spoke up about mental illness, fewer people would feel alone going through it and more people who had loved ones going through it would understand. Talking about my own depression was a step in the right direction for me. It was not easy. I was afraid and ashamed of my depression.

I took little steps. When the topic of Matt came up one day, I told a few of my closest friends about how I had been dealing with depression. I explained how I could relate to feeling that death was the only way out at times in my life. I told them how his suicide had affected me and why. Then I started to write about it in poems, essays, lyrics, and journals. From that day forward, I never stopped trying to chisel my way through my defense mechanism to expose my story and to help others.

As I headed to check in for the four-hundred-meter finals at the state that year, I thought about Matt. I pictured him walking across that indoor track with a bunch of the other guys to wish me luck as he had done the previous year. As I flashed back to that moment, it was as if he were there along with his familiar presence, and that put me at ease. Matt played a part in my journey. As I stood upon the podium to accept my third-place medal in the four-hundred-meter dash later that day, I couldn't help but smile, knowing that Matt's memory would continue to play an important role in my journey.

Chapter Sixteen

FREE FALL

Before I knew it, my senior year had arrived. I was on track to graduate with my class of 1999. I was trying to figure out where I was going to go to college. And I had started to fall down the rabbit hole of depression once again. Only this time I was more proactive because of my past experiences and losing Matt. I went to the doctor right away, and they put me on medication before it started to get worse. I had not been on medication since seventh grade. It was hard to know how to approach the situation.

The problem was that the medication only made me sicker. Here is the tricky part about antidepressants: when they are prescribed to youth, you don't really know how they will react, as their brains haven't fully developed. There are tests they can take, but for a brain that is not fully developed, there isn't any guarantee of the outcome. So doctors must be careful when prescribing medication.

Doctors are more aware of how risks in youth when prescribing antidepressants. The most efficient way to know what medications work best for a particular person is to first investigate their family tree. Have other family members had issues with mental health or had success with particular medications? If so, what age were they? It isn't guaranteed, but there's a better chance that that medication, or one in the same grouping, will be successful for that person as well.

Unfortunately, trial and error was my only choice. Mental illness runs on my father's side of the family, but there was nothing to compare my situation to. So we looked at what medication I was put on prior, and the doctor made the best decision for me.

Senior year of high school is hard for everyone. It's a year of changes. A year of major life decisions and goodbyes. It's stressful. My senior year was a time I needed focus. While I continued my medication, though, I did not care about anything. I was numb. I was not motivated. I had played basketball since I was in third grade, and that year, I quit the team. I just did not want to play anymore. In preparation for my track season, I continued to work out. I was the favorite to win the four-hundred-meter dash that year at the state meet. I had a scholarship offer for almost a full ride at South Dakota State University for track. I did not want to take it.

No matter what I did, I gained weight. I was not huge or anything, but for a track athlete bound to run in college, any weight had a major effect on me. Once the first few meets of track season started my senior year, it was clear I was not fast anymore. I could not keep up. I constantly felt lethargic and lightheaded. My coaches were in the dark. I did not tell them what was going on with me. I was afraid to. I did not want to be viewed as crazy. Even though I knew I should not be ashamed, and I knew that Matt died because of a similar situation, I still was not strong enough to openly talk about what was happening to me. I still had not fully grasped onto what my depression was or exactly what it meant for me. I also started to close myself off instead of reaching out to my friends like I had in recent years. I did not talk about my mental illness. I was numb and really did not care about much. Lots of my friends were older and graduated the year before, so I would visit them. I started to drink more socially, and mixing my medication with alcohol only made my medication not work and made me physically ill.

I kept thinking to myself that eventually my body would completely adjust to the medication like my doctor said. My parents and I talked to the doctor as my moods changed. We were told it takes up to six months to even get into the system fully.

Then I started to realize that I could not win races anymore. By the end of the year I did not even qualify for the event that I was projected to win, only for the 4 x 400-meter relay. Being a star track athlete was part of who I was my entire high school career. If I could not run fast anymore, I needed to figure out where I was going to college without running track on a scholarship.

At the time, I pretended that not going to college for track did not matter. I even started to say that running around in a little circle fast does not mean anything in the big scheme of things. But it did mean something to me. It had been part of who I was. I had loved it. That part was gone. I was devastated and was aware of that even through the numbness my medication brought on. If I was not running and part of a team, who was I?

Chapter Seventeen

THE PSYCHOTIC PSYCHIATRIST

After my freshman year of college was over, I came back home from Colorado feeling like I had not accomplished anything. That is because I literally didn't. I was still on the same medication that I started taking at the end of high school, and it still was not working for me. Instead of my body adjusting to this medication, I continued to spiral into an even worse depression. I was impulsive due to lack of emotion.

It basically made me not care about anything. The usual things I enjoyed, I completely lost interest in. I had always written poetry and lyrics, but now I did not have any desire to write. I lost my hobby of running. I was basically a walking, sedated zombie.

By the end of freshman year, I was a bigger mess than when I left. My parents decided to stop funding my idiocy, which made me think they were the Antichrist, even though it was necessary for my well-being. I did not want to come home and almost decided to stay out in Colorado and make my own way. I felt I had just started to make some new friends, and I did not want to leave them.

Fortunately, I was able to make a sensible choice and come home, despite the fact that I wasn't acknowledging the reality of how unstable I was. I was too proud to admit I was ill. I came back home and enlisted in classes at Normandale Community College while I figured out what next steps to take.

Right after I moved into an apartment with some friends back home in Minnesota, I went to a psychiatrist because I wanted to be taken off my medication. I had tried. I had let my body get adjusted to this medication, and the only thing it did was make me worse.

I remember walking into the psychiatrist's office that day. The building was open concept and made mostly of windows and wood. The sun was shining in, setting off a warm and welcoming afternoon glow. Once the psychiatrist could see me, I was escorted to his office and seated in front of his desk.

He said, "So you want to be taken off your medication?" His voice raised higher in surprise as he read my chart.

"Yes, it isn't working for me. Like I said before, it's making me worse," I said. "It makes me a zombie, and I want to feel something. I literally don't care about anything when I'm on this medication. I work out and continue to gain weight."

The psychiatrist looked at me, scratched his partially balding head, and said, "You know, you are the first person I've known that has asked to be taken off this medication."

I sat there, giving him a look, not really knowing what else to say to that. Was that supposed to make me want to stay on this horrible medication? I did not give a damn about what other people decided to do. "Well, I guess there are a lot of people that don't mind feeling nothing," I continued. "This is not treating my depression; it's overmedicating me."

He then laughed arrogantly, looked at me, and said something that I will never forget.

He said, "Well, you know medication is where the money is?"

I could not believe what he was saying. I remember I sat there in shock, wanting to yell at him but at the same time not wanting to waste my energy on him. My entire life at the time was upside down because of this medication. It was messing with my brain chemistry. That was a big deal and all he could say was "medication is where the money is"?

What should I have said? Should I have said, "Well, thank you, I am glad we cleared that up. As long as you made money off it, then that is okay. It's fine that you put an antidepressant in my body that made me worse off and suicidal"?

How many people had this guy treated? I started to feel anger burn in my stomach. I hated the thought of using medication if this were the outcome. Here I was, asking for help and not getting any. How many people had to go through trial and error for medication? How many people had to deal with this poor excuse of a psychiatrist?

I don't even know what I said in response to him. I was so upset. I think it was just a simple, sarcastic, disagreeing *yup,* because I was about to flip out. I remember feeling that this guy was acting like a teenage boy with a crush, trying to act cool around me and impress me with how much money he made.

I wanted to kick him in the balls, but instead, I acted like a professional. I wanted to get out of there and find a different doctor to help me figure out the correct medication and dosage for me.

That is exactly what I did. I left and went to my family doctor. It took a few other tries of types and dosage, but with support from my family and assistance of my family physician, I did eventually find one that worked well for me.

I never went back to that psychiatrist again, and I trusted my family physicians to help understand what prescriptions were best for me. I am not saying that psychiatrists are all like this horrible excuse for a man. What I am saying is to look out for the psychiatrist who isn't treating the entire patient.

I have since had many positive experiences with other psychiatrists. In undergraduate at University of Wisconsin–Milwaukee, I saw an amazing psychiatrist who would do my medication checks and who I would talk to for therapy. She agreed with my doctor on the type of medication. I continued with the type that my family physician had prescribed me and she adjusted dosage, but she actually was a good person who wholeheartedly cared about her patients' overall well-being.

Chapter Eighteen

THE DRIVE HOME

As I walked out of Black River Memorial Hospital, I was exhausted, but I felt a sense of hope. I also felt the best decision for me was to go home with my father and stay with family for a nice long weekend. I said my goodbyes to Nick and hoisted myself into the passenger seat of my dad's Suburban as we headed to the closest Walgreens to pick up my prescriptions before we left town.

"Honey, you can always call me," my dad said with a concerned look. "Please tell me that this is the last time you ever stop taking your medication. This has to stop."

"It is, Dad. It was just too scary to ever let it get like that again," I said.

"How is this time any different than the last times?" he asked.

I glanced out the window as we left the hospital parking lot. We passed by an old man and his wheelchair getting lifted into a bus to depart the hospital. A mother had just pulled up to the emergency area and was helping her teenage son get out of the car. He looked like he had been in an accident. His right arm was completely bandaged up, and he was cradling it with his left arm as if it were in pain. There were cuts and bruises all over his body. His knees were gashed up badly. He leaned on his mother as he limped into urgent care. If only my pain and illness were visible to the world like the teenager or the man in the wheelchair, then people would understand. I would not be sitting here trying to explain to my father what was different. He would see what was different and would not need to ask questions. I knew in my heart that I had changed. I was terrified for my life.

"Because I've never been this scared. I realize that if I don't take care of it, then I will die, and I don't want to die," I said, now with tears streaming down my cheeks.

My dad said to me, "That's just it, honey. If you take your meds and take care of yourself, you will be fine."

By the time we took the turn into the Walgreens parking lot, I was bawling with the little energy I had left. My dad handed me a tissue from his glove compartment and, after he parked, gave me a hug.

"I'll go pick up your meds and some water, Kris, and I'll be right back," my dad said.

All I could do was nod as the driver's side door slammed behind him. I flipped down the visor to catch a shocking glimpse of myself in the mirror. I did not even recognize myself. My face was blotchy, my eyes red, hair unkempt, and I had no makeup on. Maybe this time my illness was visible to people. I looked like a drug addict or a homeless bar rat. How horrible. Grandma Ellen would be so disappointed in me. Perhaps if Matt were still here, he would know what to say. Perhaps if he were sitting in the back seat, he would have the right thing to say. I let my head rest against the cool window, and I closed my eyes. I focused on my breathing and let my imagination take over.

"Hi, Kris," I heard. I turned to see Matt Pelant sitting in the back seat. Still the seventeen-year-old boy I last remember.

"Kris, you know what to do. You don't need me to tell you," he said.

"I know," I whispered, looking at his reflection in the mirror as my tears fell.

"But since you want to hear it: stop being such a dumbass and take care of yourself," he said seriously.

I started to laugh out of my cry and closed my eyes to dab them with the tissue when the sound of the driver's side door swung open and my dad climbed into the seat. I was so startled I looked behind me to see nothing.

My dad handed me a bottle of water and my prescriptions.

"Wow, a bit jumpy there, Kris? You looked like you just saw a ghost or something," he said.

I continued to look in the empty seat behind me as I said, "I guess you could say that."

"What?" my dad asked.

"Never mind," I said. "Just exhausted."

My dad started up the car and was about to put it in drive when he noticed I was sitting there staring at the pill bottles with a serious look.

"Dad, I know these pills are going to help me, but I'm nervous and afraid to take them."

By that time, my dad had taken his hand off the gearshift and turned toward me. He wanted my full attention. He was waiting for me to give him solid eye contact.

"Honey, listen to what you are saying. You are anxious to take your anxiety and depression medication?"

"Yes? I know it sounds stupid," I said.

"No, not stupid, but the way you are feeling is why you are taking the medication," he responded.

For a moment we just sat there looking at each other before we both busted out laughing.

"Good point," I said. I put both pills in my mouth and drank some water.

"Well, I am always right," my dad said, smiling as he put the car in drive.

I rolled my eyes and told him, "Well, you are right about this thing, but clearly not right about everything."

With us both laughing, my dad pulled out of the Walgreens parking lot and started to exit onto the freeway back to Minneapolis.

Chapter Nineteen

MARATHON

Many months of training, at least two eighteen-mile runs, and a solo twenty-mile run led me to the starting line of Grandma's Marathon in 2014. I am fortunate the sun is not out this summer day. Instead, it is overcast and misting rain. It is a little chilly for my liking, but I know that once the race starts, we will warm up quickly. I am lined up at the four-hour-and-fifteen-minute pacer with the teammates whom I trained with at the Lifetime Fitness in St. Louis Park, Minnesota. I listen to my playlist, which was a combination of, obviously, the complete Led Zeppelin collection and the album *Night Visions* by Imagine Dragons on shuffle. All my teammates and I are stuck in our own musical playlists as we stretch and prep for the start.

"The Star-Spangled Banner" starts up, and everyone takes off their headphones and hats to pay respect. At any race the national anthem is played, I think of my grandma Ellen and how she served our country. I think of her as inspiration and motivation. I know she is gone, but I know she is with me during every race I run. Looking over me. Cheering me on. I know that because I see her in my mother, who never misses

111

cheering me on during a race. I know it because I feel with every step I take forward in a run I am carrying on her legacy and making her proud. I am a strong woman because of her. She taught my mother to be one, and my mother taught me to be the same with every action she made in life.

Once "The Star-Spangled Banner" is over, everyone quickly puts their headphones back on and makes last-minute adjustments before the announcer starts us all out on our long morning run. It's then that I think of Matt Pelant. I think of him taking time to come wish me luck during my first state meet. I think about him before I run because he is also a part of my main motivation to run, which is that it helps me balance out my depression. It's my meditation. I know he is with me during each mile mark. Each mental struggle and success. It only seems right to take his memory with me during every race I run; after all, he was with me at that first difficult state meet.

The announcer comes over the loudspeaker and starts the countdown. After you hear the last second counted down and watch the local train in Duluth start to drive next to the runners, you wait and wait for the crowd to start moving before you can take your first step of many that day.

That first step is such a push and pull between adrenaline and the need to pace yourself. I am determined to stay with my pacer, even though as a natural-born sprinter it takes everything in me to hold back on my speed. I know if I do not take each step deliberately at the speed that I trained myself to do, then I will burn out early and not make it to the finish line. I know I have to do everything in my power to pace myself because it is inevitable that at some point between mile nineteen and mile twenty-five, I will want to give up. But I'm not going to let myself. I need every little ounce of saved energy to ensure my success of carrying on.

I feel wonderfully strong until a little after mile nineteen, and then I have to fight through some physical pain and mentally keep my body in movement to make it through. On one of the back-road miles where nobody is around, there is a man dressed as Elvis cheering all of us runners on. I am in a hard place at that moment, but the small distraction of a drunk guy dressed as Elvis cheering me on makes me briefly forget the pain in my body and pushes me further to the finish.

The most memorable moment is in that last mile, when I come around a corner to see my husband cheering me on. I am almost done. His motivation helps me get there. I recall how knowing I would see him soon kept me going and, when I see him, all the physical pain and doubt I have faced running over the last four hours vanishes. I am able to speed up as my eyes tear in complete bliss. I can see the finish line up ahead and the crowds of people cheering. I speed up for the last stretch, and as I cross the finish line, I start to tear up a bit. I did it.

As an individual puts my medal around my neck to congratulate me, all I can think about is how far I have come since that day many years ago in Black River Falls. Yes, don't get me wrong, I am more than ecstatic to finish the race, but I am even more proud of myself for making those little choices along the way to get to that finish line. It was because of those little decisions that I made it and because I was confident in myself that I would continue to be successful and happy in my life.

Chapter Twenty

THE AFTERMATH

Many years have passed since the drive to the Black River Falls hospital, but I still look back on that day for many reasons. I look back to remind myself what happens if I don't take care of myself, to remind myself how far I have come and that my mental illness can be treated with a combination of medication and taking care of my well-being.

The most important reason I look back on that day is because it was the day I acknowledged the reality of my mental illness. It was the day I made the decision to take care of my well-being. This is nothing that happened overnight. It was all about making one positive decision at a time.

First off, I never stopped taking my medication after that day. If I noticed any drastic change in how my medication was working, I'd consult a doctor immediately to adjust or change to stay ahead of any major issues with my medication.

I broke off my relationship with my long-term boyfriend Nick because it wasn't a healthy relationship for either of us. I let myself be okay with being single for a while.

I decided not to drink alcohol as much as I had been because medication mixed with excessive use of alcohol takes away from the effects of the medication and can have a negative impact on a person's mental and physical well-being.

I was able to quit smoking cigarettes. The jury has been out on cigarettes for years, but I stand by the fact that quitting was one of the hardest things I have done in my life.

I started eating healthier, and I decided to rediscover my passion for running again by joining and marathon training with the Lifetime Run team in St. Louis Park, Minnesota.

I want to note that treatment is a very personal prescription because everyone is different. Not everyone likes to run or needs medication to function. I only list the combination that works for me to give an example and reveal how I managed to tame my mental illness.

Mental illness is serious, and as a society we tend to place it in a category of its own. Much like my stepfather, John, must take his blood pressure medicine for his heart, I have to take my antidepressant to take care of my brain. We should be viewing mental illness as any other illness, not as a dreaded scarlet letter to be ashamed of and branded with.

Also, it's important to realize medication isn't used as a Band-Aid for my emotions. I may have to take my medication daily and stay ahead of my health to prevent myself from having a depressive episode, but I still must deal with the blues like anyone else. It's part of being a human being.

No one should ever be medicated for the everyday

emotions humans feel. If someone breaks your heart, you should feel hurt. If you lose a loved one, you will feel grief. It's a process to heal from these examples, and you are supposed to feel these emotions to recover. At the same time, some situational events need treatment from medication if they are taking away from a person being able to function in everyday life.

I am not a doctor, but it's important before consulting with your doctor to be aware of what you need. If you don't comprehend what you need, then how can you expect the doctor to know? Every person is different when it comes to medication, and it's all about personal balance. Take it from me, being so sedated that you can't feel anything at all opens an entire new world of issues.

After all is said and done, I have learned it's important to remind myself that I am simply human and sometimes deserve to take a break from daily routines. I am not perfect. Nobody is. We all must live life, take chances, make mistakes, and get up the next day and do it all over again. That is how we learn and grow into better people. Everyone deserves to let their hair down and enjoy life and find their own personal balance.

Today, I look around at the world we live in and believe we have come a long way with mental health treatment since I was that eight-year-old kid sitting in that giant red chair in an adult psychiatrist's office. However, I think back on Matt Pelant and others who have fallen to suicide along the way and know the world can do much better. The social stigmas associated with mental illness are still alive and strong. We as a society need to break down those barriers so that people are not afraid to reach out and get the help they need. We all need to tell our stories and own them.

Every morning I get up, take my medication, and think to myself in wonder about how much positive influence that tiny little antidepressant pill has had in my life. It saved my life. I think about how fortunate I am to be alive.

Not a day goes by that I don't reflect on the day at the Black River Falls hospital, Matt Pelant, or the others I've lost to suicide along my journey. I know Grandma Ellen is proud of me and Matt is smiling knowing that people are fighting for the other Matt Pelants of the world.

I have hope and faith that it will get better because I know it did for me—all because of my choice. Everyone has the power of choice. At the end of the day, we are all in this together, simply because we are human.

Chapter Twenty-One

A PLACE OF MY OWN

In a way, running helped save my life. The constant change that occurs in life is something we can all relate to. We all go through it. However, the most important aspect of my passion for running is that it helped me manage my clinical depression. In the days when I did not fully understand what was happening to me, it was a matter of life and death.

Fall in Minnesota is my favorite season, the time of year in which I long to run. It's when the heat of summer is coming to an end, the bitter bite of winter has not yet occurred, and spring's flower fuzz is absent from the air. My feet rhythmically hit the pavement as I jog the tar path outlined by the newly painted color palette of fall trees. Splashes of acrylic yellow paint mix into shades of oranges that coat the tips of leaves, and a candied-apple red starts to take over the lush green remains of summer. Sunlight peeks through the holes that nature created in the forest's canopy, illuminating the path before me. I can feel the warmth of the sun's rays hit my skin as I run past each ray of light. My breath is steady, and the air is crisp and clean.

This is my true vacation. Out here, my work is not present.

Organizing my five executives' schedules is not on my mind. There are no plans that I need to rush off to. Out here, I don't need to complete the balancing act with my family's calendars, attempting to remember if my stepson's basketball jersey is washed or driving my stepdaughter to play rehearsal. Calendars are not present out in the fresh air and space, where I let myself be.

My lungs crave the fall air like a drink of arctic water quenching my thirst after a long run. The coolness starts in my belly and flows through my body right down to my toes. The smashing of the dead leaves drums in time with the music playing through my headphones. The beat pulsates through my legs to my feet, motivating me to continue forward to the next mile.

Running puts me in a meditative state. The rhythm of my feet brings me into a trance and allows me to appreciate being present. It's here that I can fully let go. My pace sets in as my heartbeat picks up. Running has been an outlet for me during many stressful times in my life, like my parents' divorce, my dad moving an hour away, living between two households, my best friends moving away before fifth grade, existing on this earth as a teenager, watching my stepsiblings move away before high school and not being able to do anything about it, death, numerous heartaches, new jobs, getting married, and becoming a stepmom.

The route I take begins with a two-mile lakeside stretch where I pass by the Medicine Lake beach and playground. The wind picks up and brushes my face as I pass children who are bundled in sweatshirts laughing, playing in leaves, and tossing skipping stones in the water. I am surrounded by picnic tables and Mother Earth's loveliness until I veer left to a cement straightaway under the highway that pushes me closer to town.

Running has been a very social part of my life as well. I value and cherish those events that I have shared with coaches, friends, family, and teammates, but I prefer to run by myself. Out there on the beaten path, I never feel lonely. In fact, running alone anywhere makes me feel more connected to the world around me. I can run at my own pace. Time slows down a bit and I am aware of everything that surrounds me. I am taking it all in with each breath I take, with each desperate drink of water. For once I feel nothing but balanced. No judgment, no anger, no hurt, no stress, and no loneliness. I feel present in my body with every step I take.

The air is stagnant, and traffic is steady, leaving behind an inescapable ribbon of exhaust that lingers for the next mile. This mile is a reminder of the reality of industry. I can't help but be disgusted by the pollution and feel guilty of my own contribution at the same time. I run a bit faster to escape the odor and to calm my mind once more. I reach the edge of Brookview Golf Course, which is surrounded by lush green vegetation, allowing my lungs the refuge they need. Eventually, the path meets up with the local train tracks. I jog parallel to a very slow-moving train covered in graffiti leading the way into the industrial backyard of town that I refer to as Cement Alley.

The rusted, weathered clink of the train keeps me company and reminds me of the steady pace that life once was when it was the buzz of technology. Out here, I don't have to be constantly connected to the fast-paced evolution of technology. I don't receive hundreds of emails that I must respond to each day for work, not to mention my personal emails, the texts, Facebook, Twitter, Instagram, Snapchat, et cetera. I usually find myself overloaded and overstimulated with the constant buzz of information, and so much of this information just gets thrown at me like someone on the street handing me a flyer. So much is false news that I don't even know what is real or true anymore without extensive research. Out here, away from technology, I can disconnect and don't even think about any of these forms of communication. The only thing that I think about at that moment is being.

I am now sandwiched between the cement jungle to my right and the train to my left as it kisses the edge of the dense woods. My feet continue down the middle of the paved path that leads between two different worlds. I am close enough to be on either side, but at this moment, I go where the path leads me. No push and pull of the world; I am just passing through.

I hear the steady hum of industry as I speed by numerous workshops, factories, and warehouses. I watch workers loading heavy boxes onto semitrucks preparing to head across the country for distribution. The streak of exhaust reeks of gasoline and burning oil, as the thick, black existence invades the blue sky. My pace quickens to get away from the smoggy taste of metal that makes me cough and gasp for breath. This is the most unpleasant stretch of pavement on my route, but it's worth it to reach the other side, where nature completely takes over once again.

My feet move faster with the slightest thought of fresh air. I turn a corner downhill to reach a clearing of a park, where I ease into my comfortable pace once again. My breath becomes steady, my heart slows down, and I am at an even pace. The fresh air is nature's way of pulling me in for a hug.

The weight of the world is not holding me down. Suddenly my angry coworker who decided to take her frustrations out on me that day is forgotten, along with that man who flipped me the bird as he ran me off the road by switching two lanes. I continue past the playground, around the baseball diamonds, and run uphill to the edge of the park. By the time I reach the top of the hill exiting the park, I am grateful to the multiple cars passing by allowing me to catch my breath. Once it is safe to cross the street, I follow the path to my favorite magnificent rustic wooden bridge that appears to serve as an entrance to the woods.

Running is all about letting go of the negative thoughts and experiences that hold your body hostage with tight and cramped muscles. While I am running, my mind is clear, and that creates a space for me to figure out my personal problems and mistakes. I may not have control of much that happens in the world, but I can control my reactions. I can own up to my mistakes and correct them and try to become a better person.

As I watch the yellow finches fluttering from my position on the bridge, I can't help but wonder how many people have relied on the support of this bridge as they crossed over to the other side. How many people have stood in this exact spot, watching the beauty of nature unfold as I am at that moment? This bridge not only is a passage to the denser part of the woods, but it also represents a link to my personal escape. Once I cross into the rolling, hilly paths that wind through the thick trees, I am in Mother Nature's world.

Right before I decide to continue on my journey, I remove my headphones. In this area, the earth provides me my own soundtrack that lacks technology and industry. Each step forward brings a satisfying sound of my feet echoing off the planks of wood. A soft breeze rushes me forward as the outside world continues to melt away and I cross over into my place of comfort and solitude. A place I can call my own.

The End

Author's Notes I

MEDICATION

I deliberately chose not to include the names of medication I was prescribed to use throughout the years to treat my depression. Medication used for the treatment of mental illness is different for every patient. The type of medication that worked for me may not work for another person. The medications that caused issues for me may be the medications that work for someone else.

I was concerned that if I added the medication names, it would influence what others thought about certain medications. I am in no way an expert in psychology or qualified to be giving advice on medication.

I can only share what I have experienced through the years. One of the things I learned is that there is no way for a doctor to know how medication will affect someone whose brain isn't fully developed yet. I would suggest first asking around to find out if any relatives had success with any types of medication at an early age. What types were they? What dosage? No two people are the same, but it does give the doctors a better perspective on where to start. Chances are a person would react similarly to medication, or one in the same group, that worked for close blood relative, due to the genetic similarities.

Figuring out what type of medication and dosage can be a difficult process that shouldn't be taken lightly. After all, prescriptions dealing with mental illness are adjusting your brain chemistry. It is important for anyone trying new medications to have a support system, outside of the doctor, that is aware of the situation. That way, if a person has a bad reaction to a medication, then someone can step in and help. Especially if the person being medicated is having a bad reaction and not thinking clearly.

In a world where medication is a moneymaker, there are times when it might be abused and overused. Make sure you have the correct family doctor or psychiatrist for you prescribing medication. Question your doctor if they start prescribing prescriptions to treat the side effects of the initial prescription. Is it safe and necessary?

Prescriptions should not be used to completely numb someone. A person should still be feeling the basic human emotions. Prescriptions are used when a person's state of mind is hurting their health or not allowing them to function in everyday life.

What I mean is there are situations in life where a person needs to grieve and deal with heartache and death. That is natural. I believe that if you don't deal with situational issues, they have a way of showing up again when you least expect it. I'm not saying that some situational hardships in life don't need a temporary form of medication to go through the process, but I'm saying you can't solve situational distress with medication alone. It will help to be aware of these things.

If you are starting a new medication, I would suggest also using a daily journal to keep track of your personal progress and state of being. Sometimes side effects can be worse than the actual diagnosis and one needs a different type of medication. Also, as a person grows and develops, they might need to adjust their dosage or the type of medication entirely. When one is checking in with themselves in a journal, it is easier to be prepared and understand what medication adjustments they may need when meeting with their doctor.

SOCIAL STIGMA

Antipsychotic drugs
Mental
Crazy
Lost one's mind
Nuts
Lunatic
Unstable
Psycho
Psychotic
Lost it

These are just some of the words that are associated with mental illness. What thoughts come to mind when you read these? Anything you would want to use to describe yourself proudly?

I would say no.

I know I was afraid of what it meant to have a mental illness. There were times I was ashamed that I had to go see the head doctors. I was afraid people would think I was making it up for attention. I was afraid people would think I was nuts and stay away from me. I recall waiting for my parent's reaction to see if I was going to need to panic or not.

Social stigma keeps people from getting the help that they need. To support people in your life dealing with mental illness, I would ask you to do these things:

• When you hear someone saying negative things associated with mental health, say something. Call them out on that. It is a serious illness, and those negative comments can stick with a person.

• Listen to your friends and family. Ask questions if they seem to be in a bad place with themselves.

• If you are dealing with mental illness personally or someone you are close to is dealing with it, don't be afraid to talk about it and get the support you need.

• Talk about mental illness. Mental illness is common, and it is nothing to be ashamed of. Chances are that by talking about mental illness you will find many are dealing with the same things you are.

SUGGESTIONS

Here are some things that have worked for me when I'm having a hard day. These are things I do in addition to taking medication that is prescribed for me. These are also things you can do by yourself if you don't feel like hanging out with friends and family.

- Running

- Biking

- Writing

- Hiking

- Doing yoga

- Swimming

- Eating healthy

- Getting regular sleep

- Drinking enough water

- Avoiding alcohol unless already in a good mood

- Never drinking excessively

- Going for a walk

- Listening to music

- Biking on my Peloton or doing other exercises with instructor Emma Lovewell; her mix of musical selection and teaching fold into a powerhouse of inspiration that improves my overall wellbeing

- Reading Emma Lovewell's blog, which includes travel, healthy recipes, and little slices of inspiration

- Cleaning the house

- Doing laundry

- Watching a funny movie

- Hanging out with my dogs or cat

- Creating a playlist of songs to explain my mood

- Trying a new hobby

- Going to see a movie alone

- Having a solo dance party

- Reading one of these books:

◊ *Way of the Peaceful Warrior: A Book That Changes Lives* by Dan Millman

◊ *The Power of Now: A Guide to Spiritual Enlightenment* by Eckhart Tolle

◊ *The Electric Woman: A Memoir in Death-Defying Acts* by Tessa Fontaine

◊ *The Daily Edge: Simple Strategies to Increase Efficiency and Make an Impact Every Day* by David Horsager

◊ *The Trust Edge: How Top Leaders Gain Faster Results, Deeper Relationships, and a Stronger Bottom Line* by David Horsager

◊ *Suga Water: A Memoir* by Arshay Cooper

◊ *Boy Erased: A Memoir of Identity, Faith, and Family* by Garrard Conley

◊ *Between the World and Me* by Ta-Nehisi Coates

◊ *Letters to a Young Madman: A Memoir* by Paul Gruchow

◊ *The Year of Magical Thinking* by Joan Didion

◊ *The White Album* by Joan Didion

◊   *The Latehomecomer: A Hmong Family Memoir* by Kao Kalia Yang

◊   *The Song Poet: A Memoir of My Father* by Kao Kalia Yang

◊   *Eat Pray Love: One Woman's Search for Everything Across Italy, India, and Indonesia* by Elizabeth Gilbert

◊   *Eat Pray Love Made Me Do It: Life Journeys Inspired by the Bestselling Memoir* by Elizabeth Gilbert and various authors

◊   *Wild* by Cheryl Strayed

◊   *Tiny Beautiful Things: Advice on Love and Life from Dear Sugar* by Cheryl Strayed

◊   *The Body Keeps the Score: Brain, Mind, and Body in the Healing of Trauma* by Bessel van der Kolk, MD

◊   *All the Wild Hungers: A Season of Cooking and Cancer* by Karen Babine

◊   *Man's Search for Meaning* by Viktor E. Frankl

◊   *Madness: A Bipolar Life* by Marya Hornbacher

◊   *Dear America: Notes of an Undocumented Citizen* by Jose Antonio Vargas

Photo by Lorri Downs at yum! Kitchen and Bakery in St. Louis Park, MN

K. J. JOSEPH is an author and screenwriter. The screen-play inspired by her first book, *Simply Because We Are Human* (2021), was a quarterfinalist in the 2020 Austin Screenplay Awards, which led her to rewrite it in collaboration with screenwriter Andy Froemke under the name *A Kind of Blue*. Joseph has an MFA in creative nonfiction from Augsburg University, and has been writing and performing her work since her elementary school and undergraduate days in Milwaukee, Wisconsin. She is now based in Minneapolis, Minnesota.